I0136999

Practical Taoism
philosophy – psychology – sociology

by Prof. Myke Symonds
of
The Way of Heaven & Earth School

Traditional Taoist Arts

ISBN 10: 0-9542932-9-0

ISBN 13: 978-09542932-9-1

EAN: 9780954293291

Published by Life Force Publishing, UK.

First edition: 2022

PRACTICAL TAOISM
Philosophy - Psychology - Sociology

~

A collection of chapters,
Free ramblings of an Old Taoist.
Based upon the Philosophy of Tao
And how it interlaces with the
Everyday life sciences
Related to Mental Health
Human Welfare and Living.

With Thanks to Pre-Readers:
Bastiaan Opdenkelder (Canada)
Christos Konteas & Darren Burton
For help, suggestions and encouragement.

ISBN 10: 0-9542932-9-0

ISBN 13: 978-0-9542932-8-4

EAN: 9780954293291

Life Force Publishing
&
Life Force Books. UK.

INDEX

(Continued)

The journey to the top of the mountain
begins on rocky ground.
Starting off is hard going, and you may
stumble many times.
The climb is steep, but you can see the top.
Sometimes you may feel exhausted.
Take a deep breath and rest, then restart.
The climb may be hard, the pathway
rocky and steep, but the view from the top
is amazing. You can see all clearly before you.

FOREWORD BY THE AUTHOR

There have been many books written on Philosophy. Many deal with the Greek or more modern 'contemporary' philosophers and obviously the more commonly discussed among collegiate "intellectuals", such as Sartre, etcetera. Not much has been written on TAOist works, apart from the odd few dozen translations of the Tao Te Ching ! Of those, I would only recommend two; one by Witter Bynner (1881-1968), the other by R.L. Wing.

I hope to give you some ideas in this book as to the philosophical principles behind TAO (The Way) and what it means in terms of your life today, but in plain English. It is not meant to cover everything, merely to uncover the basics and join them together across a wider field of subject matter. This way you should be able to see their relevance and relationship more easily. What might be called mainstream Taoism is actually several branches of a tree which shares a common root. The most common form of Taoism in China seems to be liberally mixed with thoughts of Confucius and Buddhist thinking. It is the Tao of the commoner. Then we have the many Taoist Temples, recently under threat of extinction under the Communist regime, many destroyed when they came into power. Here we find a kind of Religious Taoism which usually revolves around old teachings and some minor ritual, with priesthood rankings; the Abbot being the head. Here also we find Taoist Ch'uan-shu Kung-fu, used to keep fit and usually taught alongside health and medicinal matters. Then there are the various minor branches of Taoist extremism where practitioners concentrate on sexual or life prolonging practices for a self serving purpose. This is pseudo-religion and not Real Tao. The final branches are fewer and farther between but nevertheless stronger; these are the branches Practical Taoism and are often to be seen to bear more fruits. T'ien Ti Tao Academy comes into this category. Practical Taoism is seen not just as a philosophy but a kind of Lay Science. By describing actions of life, daily happenings, health, medicine, etcetera, in terms of Tao - Yin/Yang - Wu Hsing, we can understand relationships and paths better. It helps us to build the jigsaw puzzle that is life. Often this involves the use of physical training (Taoist Kung-fu, including T'ai Chi Ch'uan), Taoist Yoga, Taoist Ch'i Kung and Traditional Chinese Medicine; built mainly on Taoist principles.

In order to discover Tao we have to go forwards and dissect the various aspects, like sayings, written verses and images that are used to portray the philosophy. In order to understand it we must then go backwards, strip it of all labels, associations and tags and simplify it to the extreme, recognising all parts as a whole. For this is the essence of Taoism, the true Way, to cut away all in your life that is not necessary and to leave whole and pure, that which just is. Many people have developed a cynical and apathetic attitude toward their daily existence. Sometimes this is just a sign of weakness, of being worn down by the modern tide of increasingly futile commercialism. This modern mayhem can be overcome with inner strength, willpower and the desire to be at One with Tao.

The ancient philosophers recognised one fundamental human truth, that we must all have a Way to follow. That way must be clearly expressed so that all can understand and appreciate its finer values. And, as we observe, in the end there is ultimately only one way which endures and lasts beyond all others - Nature's Way.

Tao and Young People
Cynicism nowadays in general society however is something bred more by recent generations from the discovery of the falsehoods which have founded our daily existence; of how much emphasis is falsely placed upon politics, fashion, industry and lifestyle. These things we can choose to accept or ignore.

•learn much more about yourself?

•learn much more about others?

•learn how to fit in with others and nature?

•become more natural and self-confident? ?

In the West it seems that intellect tries to take over from Nature. Each generation, each group or each individual tries to be more clever than the other. The Mind is a by-product of the Spirit being present in a physical body, which has a Brain so the two can interact and the body can be operated by the spirit. Here is where the problem lies. Many new people, being unaware of Tao, come to believe that their Mind is actually in charge of everything, therefore it become concerned only with the physical world. Not realising that the physical world is also Tao, they carry on to make the big mistake of ignoring Nature, the connections and the importance of the Spirit which is "fed" by Nature or Tao. This is where health and social problems begin. To use an old Taoist analogy, which I shall use probably more than once in this book, "A flower, cut off from its roots, soon withers and dies."

Only in the Taoist Arts, for it is here that you can choose to study one or as many as you wish, or not at all and just enjoy the benefits it brings to your mind and body. Whether you choose the philosophy, Ch'uan-shu Kung-fu, T'ai Chi Ch'uan, Taoist Yoga, Ch'ang Ming "Long Life" Diet or anything else, you will gain immense benefits over a life time whilst enjoying the most advanced life maintenance systems in the world, possibly the entire Universe. This is why I call it 'Practical Tao', we can use it firstly to salvage ourselves, secondly to build better understandings of the way we live and thirdly to heal, mend, become stronger or just live more peacefully; Wu Wei.

The author has studied psychology, philosophy, observed social behaviours (Sociology), diet and related health/illness/mentality, plus the main Taoist Arts; Taijiquan, Qigong, Gongfu, K'ai men and TCM. Through this and other studies of other ancient Eastern Arts, many spiritual experiences have been had. Just one of these was the creation of the verse below. Whilst sitting on a sofa, doing something else, my spirit was guided by a unseen, unheard presence. This led to packing up what I was doing, walking past the computer and switching it on; but I knew not why, for I had no intent to do anything on it at all! Having had many such guided experiences, I accepted it. Made a cup of Tea and sat in front of the screen wondering what I was there to do. The unseen, unheard force directed me to fire-up the Word Processor programme, so I did. Bemused still, I sat there looking at blank new page. Then suddenly these words started to flow into mind and out through my fingertips, without hesitation, without thought. Only when it was finished did I read what was written. Then I understood not only the importance of what was said, but that it was part of my life's work here, with the pure Taoist Arts.

The TAO has no name, no form.

No words can describe it, so vast is The Way,

So immense The Universe.

From inaction comes action.

The Tao is action.

Action has no fixed form.

Form has creation.

Creation has meaning.

The Way is my tool.

I am a tool of The Way.

Where Tao cannot be heard,

Then I am its voice.

Where Tao cannot be seen,

I can paint an image.

Where Tao cannot be touched,

I can touch and be touched.

Where words fall upon the ears.

And then fade away,

Ink flows to paper,

And words stay.

Tao is there for everyone.

Tao has much to say!

'The Unwritten Verse' of the Tao Te Ching by Lao Tzu

Scribed through Myke Symonds, February 1995.

In retrospect, I have analysed this, believing that Lao Tzu was indeed a wonderful man who was profoundly in touch with Tao, the Universe. However, his much translated works only accredits Tao, even though the Taoist Philosophy is connecting the great Triad; Heaven, Earth and Man. Lao Tzu was a "tool of the way", just as I am, and many others too. With my hand on my heart, I can honestly say that my whole life has been "driven", my Path or Way marked out for me, with no escape; and I have tried to change lifestyles but always got pushed back to Taoist Arts, teaching, helping, healing and, of course, writing. What happened to Lao Tzu as he was leaving China was preordained too. He could not escape his destiny. None of us can.

During the course of this book, I shall let Tao guide me as I write about my studies, findings and theories based upon them. The ultimate is Tao, hence names as " T'ai Chi " in the amazing Art of T'ai Chi Ch'uan – Supreme Ultimate Boxing; T'ai Chi meaning Tao, the Supreme Ultimate. For those of you who do not know already, T'ai chi Ch'uan, or modern Taijiquan, is an exercise form based on self-defence, first developed by a man called Ch'eung Sam Feng (born April 9th 1247; also written as Zhang Sanfeng; also spelled Zhang San Feng, Chang San-Feng). He moved on to study Tao and Taoism, and through his journeys met the right people and learned the right things to move him forwards to his life's goal. He achieved that goal by developing something we think was called "36 Methods Boxing", was a fluid or "joined-up" Form of movement, but more importantly, used the philosophical images and guidelines of Taoism. Hence, if you learn Taijiquan, this should be combined with suitable Qigong, and use those same guidelines.

Preamble over, introductions made, let the rest of this little book take shape. It has been a very long time's work, meditations, studies, adventures, discoveries and hardships, failures, successes, spiritual journeys, and much, much more, but this is my Way.

In a dream or vision many years ago I was shown a series of books, all with a similar cover to this one, and covering the main aspects of Taoist Studies. These are "traditional", not formalised Arts. They are "pure", not commercial. These studies derive from the many twists and turns in my life's pathway and the many experiences, positive and negative, the teachers and healers I have met, and much, much more. It is all just "life on Earth", the Triad of Heaven, Earth and Man.

Finally, it is my hope that by pointing out the many connections of Taoist philosophy and every day practical living, social and psychological issues, potential fixes, plus psychological values included, that this will inspire some of you to change things for the better. The one thing which really needs to be changed is what most call "the System", which is usually fixed, doggedly outdated, out of touch and tries to make people of all hypothetical shapes fit it, rather than *it* fitting the purpose they have need for. The System tries to pigeonhole people who just won't fit in limited boxes; make more boxes and you just create more problems. We need to simplify, include, not exclude, make deviations normal, not abnormal. We do not criticise one flower for being different to the other 300 Million, so why should we do so with people?

Blessings. May Tao be kind to you.

Myke

Shih-fu Myke Symonds – Grandmaster of T'ien Ti Tao P'ai (The Way of heaven & Earth School of Traditional Taoist Arts.)

CHAPTER ONE:

WHAT IS TAO ?

"What is TAO?" The simplest answer to that question would be, "everything". However, for now let us have a look at The Tao in some detail; we can break it down into origins, principles and basic building blocks. Each aspect may then be clearer to our Minds and the subject of each chapter should then be 'naturally' linked by the process of understanding.

TAO: a Chinese word (pronounced, "Dow") which, in basic translation means; Way, Truth, or Path.

The precise translation of the Calligraphic symbol within Chinese texts would only be found by searching for its context within the sentence or story in which it appeared. Otherwise, by itself, it may be taken as reference to 'The Way', as in Tao Te Ching, 'The Way of Nature' by Lao Tzu; also Way of the Universe. In the West we often refer to the "Nature" of things. Taoism has gained two main sorts of follower since its appearance as a philosophy. One, the devotee/alchemist type and the other, the more casual follower/observer type. Essentially Taoism is a philosophy rather than a religion. This is always a sticking point: For example, Christ was not a Christian and did not apparently ask for a religion to be founded in his name, but his philosophy was segmented, fragmented and reformed differently evolving into a devotee (religious) practice called 'Christianity' (even though some forms of this bear no resemblance to what we are led to believe that Jesus himself practised, from Biblical translations). Buddhism, Taoism, et cetera, have all suffered similar fates at some time or stage. I believe that originally Tao was a simplified, lay-science which was semi-pictographic – using images such as Yin/Yang symbol - related to those people (many of whom may have been unable to read and write) who simply desired a more natural lifestyle, or to understand that which they had already. These folk probably wanted nothing more, in times of unrest, poverty and hard rule (not unlike today!), than to live in harmony with Nature. There are millions of people all around the world today and always shall be, whose dream it is to live in a little country cottage, surrounded by the realities of Nature... has anything really changed!

道 - TAO (pronounced "Dow")

Chinese does not translate accurately into English as the calligraphy is 'pictograph': it is a graphic symbol or image of a word, name or meaning. The nearest translation of TAO is 'WAY', however this can change according to the context of the sentence it is put into, so therefore could mean 'Path', but the literal translation from traditional Mandarin Chinese is 'Way' or 'Truth' but can also mean 'Path' as the two ancient pictographs it is made up from represent 'head' and 'walk' which may be translated as "journey of consciousness". Chinese calligraphy, pre-modern Simplified, can mean different things according to the context of the sentence or surrounding characters.

What does this mean?

Tao or Way refers to the entire Universe. The Universe is too big to imagine or know fully, but being in one tiny part of it on our World (Earth) we can see the actions of the Way all around us. This we call 'Nature' and also 'Natural Phenomenon'. Tao is everything in the Universe, all substance, all matter and anti-matter, all planets, life and even dust. Tao is everything and the way that existence happens, creation, birth, life, death, interaction and even non-action (stillness).

My Old Master, Prof. C. Chee Soo, had this to say about Tao:

"Always remember that Taoism is *not* a religion, for it encompasses all beliefs and religions, for it came into being more than 10,000 years B.C. It is a way of living in accordance with the energies of the universe, and following the ordained WAY of life as laid down by TAO".
(Extract from 'The Tao of My Thoughts' by Chee Soo – Published by Seahorse Books. ISBN 095424454) Author's Note: This is a lovely book, written naturally with his thoughts as they happened. He also penned several other books on the Taoist Arts, a couple which I have tried to expand on and make a wider appeal for; such as T'ai chi Diet.

The Concept of Tao

The concept of Taoism as a common practice for the people was purportedly founded by The Yellow Lord, Huang Ti [2697 - 2597 B.C.]. The period in which he reigned as the third of the first five Chinese rulers, is called 'The Legendary Period' [2852 - 2205 B.C.]. His personal name was said to be Yu-hsiung [1], while his surname was Chi (after the River by which he was born). His Mother was Fu Pao. Chi Yu-hsiung (Huang Ti) was also responsible for important research into medical matters.[2] He was probably the best so-called "Ruler" that this tiny planet has ever seen.

Generally speaking, Taoism accepts all that happens within the Universe as being natural phenomena. As day and night exist side-by-side, so too, for example, good and evil must exist. Taoism does not attempt to dictate. So those who practice the 'dark arts' are not called unholy, inhuman or demonic. Equally it does not praise those who practice only the 'white arts' as being pure or angelic. Such affairs are seen as transitional - as a natural part of the whole. All things exist and therefore are accepted. In some Taoist Temples you will see this recognition that all things are of the same creator, images of Christ and the Devil beside Lao Tzu, evil demons beside the Goddess of mercy and so on. But here is a point, should there be any Taoist "Temples"? The reason for this question is that Tao is essentially a simple concept - not, as said earlier, a religion - concepts do not have Temples, idiosyncrasies and worshippers, concepts are just ideas or expressions. Temples, idols, carved or painted images, tokens and talismans are just a simple, physical expression of a mental notion, like a museum or art gallery. The statue of the enchanting and enigmatic Venus is one such physical expression, but we do not worship her as a religious icon. People who worship religiously, for want of a better word, are usually unable to attain true Oneness with the Universe. They lack the ability to see clearly what life is, so the adoration of some eulogised figurehead, one who has or purportedly has achieved "great and mysterious things" becomes their habit. Their habit becomes ritualised and the rituals become more important than the art of living a balanced and natural life, in harmony with all nature. To be clear, the word "temples", like the word "religion" is something that unknowing Western minds have labelled them, not Taoists. To a Taoist, it is just

---

[1]   His name was also Hsien-yuan (the name of the village by which he dwelt, say some. Others say this refers to Wheeled Vehicles, Pottery, Ships and Armour, et cetera - things he allegedly invented)
[2]

a place to go and study, meditate or be inspired by images and figures. To western minds they may look like churches.

The understanding of all these concepts must not be "jumped at" or grabbed too quickly. One should contemplate the meaning and slowly it becomes clear, as the settling of mud in a pool allows clear vision to the bottom, in time.

In the Orient, where Taoism was conceived, there have been many sects of Taoists, from those who wish to lead the simplest of lives in accordance with nature, to those who practice some ritual with 'talisman' and charms to bring 'luck', through to those who practice within one or other of the more questionable secular activities. These include sexual exercises, such as gaining pleasure for oneself and neglecting your partner's needs - a quite unnatural practice. One sect supposedly attains 'higher states' by having sex with as many partners as possible, for instance; a female will have as many younger men as possible, bringing each to climax and absorbing their Yang energy without releasing her own Yin energy in return. Likewise, a male might have as many younger women as possible to gain their Yin energy without letting go of his own Yang energy. These sort of practices looked at from a psychological viewpoint would tend to imply some sort of repression and not rally the actions of a 'well balanced' person. These images seem typical of people who will grab at a philosophical or religious notion which appeases their self-gratuitous senses in some way, be it physically or psychologically.

For or Against?

To go against nature, to worship idols, practice ritual magic, gratuitously self-indulge or become religious or in any fixed way is NOT the TRUE WAY of the Universe. For the Universe is full of interaction, it has many forces, each of which have cause and effect, none are separate but they are part of the whole. Nature is perfect, even though it might appear to "interfere" with man kinds' plans at times, it is mankind that is interfering. It is only when we rid ourselves of these pre-conceptual ties and bonds that we can become enlightened.

Confucius, another of China's philosophic sons, said that no man should turn his beliefs into a religion or cult. It is a shame that those who have perverted and bastardised Taoism did not see clearly why Lao Tzu (sometimes spelt, Lao Tsu) did not wish to write down his philosophy in the first place! Let us look at the first verse of 'Lao Tzu's 'Tao Te Ching' (The Way of Life) - this translation by an American author and student of The Way, R.L. WING;

The Tao that can be expressed

    Is not the Tao of the Absolute.

The name that can be named

    Is not the name of the Absolute.

The nameless originated Heaven and Earth.

The named is the Mother of All Things.

Thus, without expectation,

    One will always perceive the subtlety;

And, with expectation,

    One will always perceive the boundary.

The source of these two is identical,

    Yet their names are different.

Together they are called profound,

    Profound and mysterious,

The gateway to Collective Subtlety

What this first verse tells us is that the original creations had no name and that no words can adequately describe them (Tao is so vast that no one name is possible, that's why we humans call it the "Universe"). It goes on to tell us that we should not try to intellectualise or try to perceive, otherwise we would be frustrated; for if you expect one thing and that does not appear, then you may get confused by that non-appearance of that which you expected.

Finding Tao is a personal thing, something which can only be experienced in time, not hurried or made falsely. So, what exactly is TAO ? It is everything and nothing, the way that day exchanges constantly with night, Winter with Summer, birth into death, death into life and the way that men and women are different yet the same, the way that birds migrate and the rivers run to the sea. It is all things, great and small, all things natural and in keeping with Nature. For once we forget our own natural instincts or conscience, then we have at that moment lost touch with Tao.

Tao is the entire Universe or Multiverses, including everything in them, planets, gasses, dust, animals, humans, other "alien" life forms, the Galaxies and everything that you can see, touch, hear and feel, plus much more that you, and others, have as yet to discover.

In Summary.

Tao is the Ultimate Reality. The supreme being is beyond words, we only use the word Tao to let others know what we are talking about, otherwise it is nameless, shapeless, beyond description and understanding. We, as humans, can see and feel the effects of Tao. The name "Tao" has been used to describe the entire workings of the Universe, various other names are used to describe parts of Tao, like Yin and Yang, the two main forces or actions.

What is Taoism? 道 教

Taoism (pron. as "Dow-izm") is the practice of following Tao or trying to understand it.

This is a philosophy developed by mankind, using the observed processes of the Universe as guidelines to develop oneself in a way which is more harmonious to Nature. This is why we use the Triad of Heaven (Creator), Earth (physical Mother of life forms on earth) and

Man (humanist life forms.) Taoism is an educational system whereby we can use the guidelines, such as the Daodejing, to guide us into a more natural and harmonious lifestyle, with better health and enlightenment.

It is not altogether surprising that in this world, today, with all of its "plastic" (to coin a phrase of the sixties) distractions that we should loose touch with Tao at some time or another. But to many it is a vague and shrouded childhood memory of feelings; no words, no labels, oneness, feelings of wonder and discovery. I remember these things but became semi-detached whilst being 'educated' in the sciences of fractions and labels. But now I am trying to "unlearn", you might say, to return to that wonderful primordial state of just being. Oh, the simplicity and beauty of early childhood! Let your child within you and your offspring discover and play with Nature, content it's heart with the wonders that it sees so clearly, those that your burdened adult mind may have forgotten. Do not try to put your adult worries on those small shoulders, for fear of breaking their back. Let Nature be.

Should you be one of the (so many!) unhappy souls who, either physically or mentally, were abused in your youth or in relationships, and carry the scars on your mind, which reflect in your relationships, or carry hatred in your hearts, let it go. Try to find it in your hearts to forgive those who sinned against you, for they lost The Way and were confused. Accept that no-one is perfect and let the driving force in your heart be the desire to become balanced and harmonious. See how Nature heals a trail of destruction in a forest by turning old into new and planting seeds for growth and expansion. Then, by example, you will be able to show others The True Way.

In short, Taoist philosophy is about;

   •Learning what is natural and what is unnatural.

   •Simplicity: Living simply,being pure or natural, not fake.

   •Complicity: Following 'True Nature' and understanding life.

   •Learning to live with Nature, not going against it.

   •Alchemy: Turning something plain into something very special.

Others may describe this differently, but that is fine. We all communicate in different ways.

Taoism is possibly the largest study or following in the world, with Buddhism second and Christianity (in its many forms) tagging on in third place. Why? That is something that you can meditate on yourself, my job is just to tell you about Tao and Taoism.

A person wishing to understand Tao may observe Nature, take part in exercises which follow Taoist principles, like Taijiquan (pronounced "Tie-chee-chew-aan") and even meditations. The written guidelines are studied and the relationship between Tao and the person's life are studied and evaluated. As impossible as it may seem to develop mentally from a physical exercise, or so it seems at first, Arts like T'ai Chi Ch'uan do have a very profound effect on not only the body, but the Mind and the Psyche too. A good teacher will be able to spot where you are "imbalanced" by the way you move or stand, so transforming the physical, which then has an effect on the relationship between body, energy and Mind. Hence there is a saying in Taoist Arts that they practice "alchemy", thus transforming "lead into gold".

Observant readers will notice that on this, and my other book covers in this series, is a bar design at the top. This represents Lead with Gold above it. Therefore it is a symbol of turning lead into gold, or "transformation", not of metals, but of the Soul.

Look at the author's posture in this movement from Tiaji Dao (a more advanced form of Taijiquan that is learned after Open Hand and Staff 'Kun' Forms.) See the symmetry of posture? Note the "opening" of the body, with twisting: all these varied movement aid far better health through transformations within.

The Arts of T'ai Chi Ch'uan, Chi Kung and all other Taoist Arts for healthy exercise, all feature movements which involve better posture, twisting the waist and breathing correctly; we call them "Arts" as they are of a high level, like a that of a great painting Artist, or Dance Artist, someone who has trained for many years to reach high-level skills. Each one of these Arts has taken years to develop, often with accumulated input from wide afield and other very knowledgeable and experienced people. This can be compared with what is happening a lot in the West with general exercises, for there are many individuals who try to take bits and pieces of exercise routines, then create something "new", so that they can be the "sole proprietor" of it and claim accolade. The Taoist Arts are collective and have always been that way, no matter which teacher may advertise his or her classes under their own banner.

Harmony.

Many wise people, today and as far back as when humans started thinking, realise that to achieve anything useful in life you need to work together with other people. The reasons for this breech both the physical and the psychological. One person can be helped in exercise, skill learning or other physical tasks, by another who already has these skills. From a psychological viewpoint, people may think or see things in a slightly different way, so solving problems can become easier if tackling it from two angles instead of one. Just pause and think of times in your life you had help with something, especially when younger and before you were taught how to do things for yourself. This is Teamwork.

Even the loneliest recluse on the planet has to rely on teamwork. Unless they build a house completely from scratch, they would have to buy or trade for materials, food, clothing, lighting and heating, tools and more. All of these things were made or gathered by more than one person, through teamwork. Such things are often taken for granted as someone these days can just pop into a supermarket and get what they want. This reminds me of an old story that was told by an old school teacher, from the days when big cities like Sheffield (England) was a major steelworks city, lots of smoke, ash dust and crammed housing. A man is Sheffield had never been outside the city, so had never seen the countryside or a farm. He was asked "Where do apples come from?" His reply was "On a stall." He apparently had no idea that they grew on a tree, in an orchard and on a farm. When I was a lad I was walking along the beach one day. I saw a solitary man just standing by the shoreline, staring left and right out to sea. As I approached, I could see he looked bewildered. Not knowing if he was lost, or had issues, I asked if he was alright. "Aye lad." he replied, but then raised his hand and pointed to the far left-to-right, "But what is that?" he enquired. I looked at the sea and saw nothing unusual, no ships, seals or other objects. "What's what?" I asked him. "That (he pointed)... that sort of curved line in the distance?" I looked, "Ah! The Horizon." He looked astonished. "Horizon?" he quizzed. "Yes," I answered, "it's where the Earth curves and is as far as we can see. Beyond that is Holland and France over that way." The man was speechless for a moment, then said, "Oh, thanks. I've never seen that before!"

Seems incredible that someone had never seen a wide-open space before, and had never been out of a big city before, so had no idea what the Horizon was. There are many instances in life when someone has seen or experienced something that you have not. Therefore, sharing knowledge can broaden your mind, or day I say "new horizons"?!

Nobody knows exactly how Taoism came about, but it would be a shrewd guess to say that someone watched Nature and decided that it was the most powerful and prolific force known to mankind. Then they shared their thoughts with another, or others, who were similarly inclined. This is how we progress in our life and education. This is why we read books. Anyone who has not read books has not broadened their horizons, and may have a very narrow view of life.

It must be realised that the world is a far bigger place and that your own experiences are as small as one grain of sand on all the beaches in the world. Not only that, there are billions of others who have walked on this planet before you, billions and billions. They have all had experiences, some quite unique. Those who have written about their experiences and shared them freely, may have helped someone else have a better life, or at least a better understanding of it.

The study of Tao, "Taoism", has many unique and wise guidelines that have been established by others to make "finding the Way" easier for those who follow.

The Three Treasures.

The "Three Jewels" improve the quality of life. A Taoist will try to live by these codes of conduct. They are:

1. Compassion, kindness and gentleness. These can be translated many ways, but generally imply being good to others, not harming anyone and caring for others.

2. Frugality, charity and moderation. Mostly these speak for themselves. Being kind, giving without thought of reward, being "sparing" yet giving just enough, moderation in all things and not being excessive.

3. Not daring to be first in the world. Ego, often the downfall of many a human, is something to be kept under control. Do not desire to be first, but strive to complete your life in the best way possible.

Together, The Three Treasures, they make for better morals and less aggravation within society. By developing harmony with teamwork, we can make any load lighter and any journey more affable.

How does this deal with the perceived need to compete, to be better than others in order to make a living? The answer to that is inside yourself. The "ideal" in Taoism is not to compete, but to make yourself as good as you possibly can be. If you do that, in your chosen career or way of life, then there is no need to compete. By being as good as you can be, you will be a great person to deal with, and offer a really efficient and friendly service, with a conscientious eye to detail. That will set you apart from those who set-up a false image just to make money! There are also those who have mental health issues, caused by someone else in their life, but which they will reflect on you ("Transference"). Try to avoid situations which may be abrasive or destructive.

"Do as you would be done by."

Taoist Philosophy

The philosophy of Tao was written many years ago and created by many thousands, if not millions, of Taoists. Perhaps the most notable are Lao Tzu and Huang Ti.

Huang-Ti ("Huang-di") - The Yellow Emperor(黄帝)

Huang-di, the Yellow Emperor, is a legendary Chinese sovereign and a popular cultural hero who is considered in Chinese mythology to be the ancestor of all the Han Chinese. Huang-di reigned from 2497 BCE to 2398 BCE. His personal or family given name was said to be Gōngsūn Xuānyuán (公孙轩辕). Huang-di was hailed as a chief deity of Taoism during the Han Dynasty (202 BCE-220 CE)1.

Huang-di became very interested in Tao and its principles. He gathered as much information from across China as he could; an incredible task, considering there was no postal service, radio or television and very few books in those times. The Emperor selected Five Personal Advisers (three woman and two men) who were responsible for collecting or evaluating facts. They looked into every aspect of life, from diet and health to marriage and relationships, to living and dying.

Among many accomplishments, Huang-di has been accredited with "The Yellow Emperor's Canon of Internal Medicine". The Huang-di Neijing (黄帝内經), said to be authored in collaboration with his physician Qibo ("Chee-bo"); some modern historians think it was compiled from ancient sources by a scholar living between the Zhou and Han dynasties, more than 2,000 years later and some now believe that Qibo was in fact Hippocrates (ca. 460 BC – ca. 370 BC): believed to be the author of the Hippocratic Oath, which Doctors swear by to this day.

Huang-di's interest in natural health and preventing and treating diseases, according to historical sources, meant he lived to the age of 100, and attained immortality after his physical death. Huang-di is an important figure in Chinese religions, particularly Taoism and Confucianism. He introduced the earliest form of formalised Martial

Arts into China, because he was also good in medicine, he knew that Martial Art was beneficial for both good health and self-defence.

Huang-Ti is said to have ruled for 100 years, had 25 children, 14 of whom were sons. Of these 14 sons, 12 chose last names for themselves. It is also said that all the noble families of the first 3 dynasties of China, Xia, Shang and Zhou were all direct descendants of Huang-di. The Korean descendant of Huang-di include the family Paik of Suwon region in Korea (other possible transliteration: Baik, Back, Paek, Beak, Paek, Baek) or (Korean 水原 白氏) and the first figure to arise as a self-identified Korean is Woo-Kyung Paik or (松溪公白宇經).

When Huang-di had lived for over 100 years, he arranged his worldly affairs with his ministers, and prepared for his journey to the Heavens. One version said a Dragon came down from the Heaven and took Huang-di away. Another version said Huang-di himself turned into half-man and half Dragon and flew away.

Huang-di, through his study and help of his Five Personal Advisers who collated information from all over China, is accredited with laying the first organised foundations of Taoist belief. He also commissioned and possibly even took part in the design of many inventions. Overall he was a highly intelligent man and remains a worthy and highly respected icon of Chinese history; and should really be included in world-wide schools history lessons.

His contribution to his land, the people in it, their lives, was enormous. His book lives on to this day and is still the "gold standard" in health education for TCM; and would help all other health systems too. It is not known factually by the author, but at an educated guess I would say that it was possibly he who used the superbly simple graphics associated with Taoism, such as the Yin/Yang symbol. With such simple tools you could explain to those who could not read about seasonal changes, farming, relationships, and much more besides. To those who were medically inclined, the images are useful in showing how one situation affects another. To those who practice and develop the health related exercise skills, or even Ch'uan-shu ("Kung-fu": *slang*) these images could explain many interactions.

However, and as always, books and education leads to scholars, and occasionally, a Great Scholar; someone who not only understands, but can see and relate the subject to everyday life. In this case, Lao Tsu, who so poetically translated his studies of life (sociology) and people's actions (psychology) into the everlasting verses that we know of as Tao Te Ch'ing or Daodejing.

An Artist's image of Lao Tzu

CHAPTER TWO:

THE TAO & LAO TZU (Lao T'zi)

Like most of China's historic characters, Lao Tzu is mostly legendary. That is to say that his tales are passed down from century through century orally and in other writings. Much of china's early records and books have either been lost or deliberately destroyed. This is very unfortunate as there is so much to be of interest to so many. However, this is not an uncommon fate, as it has happened in Egypt, Syria, Tibet and even here in England. The wisdom of the ancients has been returned to dust, but because mankind has a need for knowledge and enlightenment, most of the knowledge has been passed forwards through many generations and great teachers.

Lao Tzu's philosophical translations of the Tao are somewhat different. Such an impact did his writings and beliefs have, that they have survived virtually intact and still as clear as a Mountain Stream and as refreshing in their truthful simplicity; whether or not they have been added to over the centuries. There has, since 1946, been some critics from within China who are said to be historians, and who have publicly said that the found bamboo scrolls were not the originals, that they were some other scholar's translations, etc. My point of view, which I try to maintain as logical, asks why would a secondary person create then *hide* his scrolls? For if they were only his opinion of the matter, then there would be nothing special about them.

Contrary to this, if, for example, the infamous gatekeeper considered these his "real treasures", then yes, why not bury or hide them so that they did not get stolen or lost while he was at work. Since 1946, a critical year in China's turbulent history, there have been many changes, many folklore tales changed, many a book destroyed and many a traditional thinker suddenly taken or "vanished" at night and, according to some, killed or had vital organs removed while still alive; later sold to "rich" Communist supporters!

History cannot be rewritten as the true history is always preserved by someone, somewhere and in some form. Scholars of TAO have no need to deny, doubt or rearrange things, they just study and evaluate all knowledge with what they already have and go forwards.

Lao Tzu.

Lao Tzu was said in folklore to have been immaculately conceived by a shooting-star and then carried in his Mother's womb for sixty-two years'. When he was born, it is said that he already had white hair and a beard! The year of his birth is recorded as 604 B.C. Not much is known about his earlier life, like most legendary figures.

It is known that after some time he became the Keeper of the Imperial Archives at Loyang, an ancient capital in what is now the Province of Honan (home Province of the famous Son Shan, Shaolin Temple). At one time during his role as philosophical advisor he was visited by another legendary character, Confucius. He wished to ask Lao Tzu's advice on certain points of etiquette and ceremony. Lao Tzu had little time for such 'false' matters and deemed it all nonsense and hypocrisy! Confucius was baffled by the older man and his ways of speaking of the affairs of mankind. Baffled, he returned to his own disciples whereupon he said that Lao Tzu was a mysterious and great man who was equal to Dragons (a fine compliment).

It is said that much of his adult life was spent in trying to educate people who were interested in the philosophy of Tao. He had a few good friends who would meet with him to discuss various points they had considered. Generally he was respected, but as with all humans, throughout history and still today, there will always be the odd one or two who criticise, him, me or you. This is natural, this is the Way of Humans. Social Media (what a contradictory title!) is renown for these people who just love to put down someone else with abrasive or undermining comments; they are known as "Keyboard Warriors; people who hide in semi-anonymity and practice negativity.) However, these people are irrelevant for your intents or purposes, as it is what you do that counts. Always remember that.

An old analogy that is often used in teaching Tao or life matters in general is that of a ripple; e.g. You drop a pebble into a still pond, then watch the ripples surge outwards from the centre to the edges. Whatever you do in life is like that stone. It may sink to the bottom of the pond, create a small disturbance in the mud, which later settles, but those ripples, they carry on a bit longer. If yo do something negative or "nasty" in life, the action creates proverbial ripples. This may be a chain of gossip, misinformation, character assassination or even something far more harmful, such as a mental health damage condition like PTSD. The ripples in life may not be seen, but most certainly can be felt by those affected.

For these reasons, the use of positive imagery or Confucian type morals have been interlaced into the fabric of the Taoist philosophy. Every philosophy must have guidelines for character development. Creating and maintaining a positive environment is essential to world development. Unless we learn to be good to each other, spread positive actions, then life would be too miserable to bear for most. Having said that, there will always be Yin/Yang. Yang is positive, so we look towards growth, light and illumination, but within a Yin or peaceful and harmonious environment. Yet there are other beliefs out there in this world, one which practises negativity, hatred towards anyone different, death to those who disagree, plus defiling women of a non-native to their own country, just to "spoil" them Some practice other forms of hatred, murder and abuse in the name of their beliefs; another form of Yang actions, but this time in a Yin (negative) manner, creating a more Yin or negative environment. This is where we view balance or unbalance, harmony or disharmony.

Lao Tzu was well educated and well studied. Therefore he could see disharmonious circumstances clearly, his clear and free-thinking mind able to decipher the causing parts in a short burst of clear thought. By studying that which is clear, natural and true, you can develop to spot that which is false, unnatural or fake likewise. We do not have to look for it, it just happens; like learning that an object is light in weight automatically makes us decide that another object is heavy. This is not judgement. It is clarity and automatic recognition. So those who learn to think become unthinking. Tao does not think, therefore "unthinking" is as spontaneous as Tao.

Toward Lao Tzu's Autumn years he became tired and saddened by people's tragic indisposition to simply accept their miserable and false ways of life and to live with natural goodness and an integral respect for life (Nature), and each other. He decided to travel away from, so called , "civilisation" and leave China and so rode off on a water buffalo, hoping to settle where he was not known and would therefore be left in peace. As he reached one of the gates of the Great Wall, another monument of his era, a gate-keeper by the name of Yin Hsi stopped him. It seems that Yin Hsi had recognised him from a precognitive dream which told of the great philosopher's coming. Yin Hsi told him of this dream and somehow persuaded Lao Tzu to stay for a while as his guest while writing his thoughts on Tao. The traveller, riding an old Ox, was weary, so was persuaded to stay and rest. It was during that stay, it is said, that Lao Tzu wrote the verses now known as the Tao Te Ching or Daodejing – The Way of life.

It is just as well that Yin Hsi, according to the legend, was able to be so persuasive and get Lao Tzu to stay over and rest, as without his interaction there may never have been such a great, honest and wise classic as the Tao Te Ching. It seemed very unlikely that Lao Tzu would have recorded anything otherwise, as he was a very quiet man who believed that the way to do was to be. He was not one to put himself forward publicly or socially, nor as a scholar - he was anti-scholastic, in fact, and considered scholars to be as blinkered as their tutors! (I agree, Old Teacher, those who follow blindly remain blind!)

This is echoed within the Tao Te Ching. Nothing is known about the death of Lao Tzu, where or when. It is thought that he crossed the border to India, but no records remain.

Translation of Daodejing:

Tao   = The Way, Way, Path, Truth.

Te   = Power, Universal workings.

Ching = Classic.

Tao Te Ch'ing - Pronounced as; Dow De Jing (Sometimes, Dow Deh Jing which are just ways of writing in ways that the words are pronounced.)

Because each word of the Chinese origin can have more than one meaning the context can change according to the sentence in which it is used. If someone spoke of the existence of a book which offered an explanation to life's forces, then it may be taken as "Classic

(writings and observations) of The Way of Universal workings".
Otherwise it could be read as "The Way of Power", "The Truth of
Power", etcetera; power being taken as the powers of Nature, the
driving force of the Universe which is uncontrollable and unstoppable.

In a more narrow or localised sense, looking at it from a resident of
this planet's point of view, we refer to it as "The Way of Heaven and
Earth", which is the name by which our Taoist Kuoshu (traditional
Chinese Arts) Academy is known – Website URL:
www.TTTkungfu.com

The Way.

Tao is the intellectual translation of the energy, physical
and metaphysical powers of the the Universe. Noted by
great observers and translated into practical applications
by great men and women; of far more importance than
most western philosophers and inventors who are given
higher status, for some warped reason. Tao and Taoism
has real practical values and can be used to make people's lives
happier, safer and more free of worry. It could be used to improve
society; as this begins at home. In fact, that was exactly what
happened under the auspices of The Yellow Emperor, Huang-di or
Huang-Ti. He elected Five Aids; 3 women and two men. He
discussed everything with them. They also had people they would
relate to, and who would in turn relate to the outer offices, who were
in touch with the general public. Hence, nothing was done without
considering how the general public would feel about any changes.

Huang-di sent emissaries out across the wide continent of China.
They were tasked to find any information about Taoism that they
could and bring it back to Huang Ti and his five advisors. Can you
imagine, with the size of China, no transport systems like we have
today, no borders with Korea, what an enormous task that was to
undertake? Eventually, they returned with information. The Emperor
studied it, consulting with his team, getting different opinions and their
translations of the subject. This must have taken an enormous
amount of time and energy of a full day, day after day, after day.
Perhaps many younger people today do not realise how lucky they
are having access to already stored information.

35

Eventually, The Yellow Emperor announced the "arrival" of the Taoist philosophy. He showed the people how they could improve their agriculture methods, improve their marriages, relationships or lifestyles generally. He made Taoist Health Practices more widely known and available, delivering TCM to the general public. He made enormous changes and was rightly hailed as a truly wise and great leader. It is his type of leadership that Lao Tzu refers to in his Daodejing, when he says "A poor leader enslaves people. Therefore they rebel. A wise leader sets people free, therefore they follow him." How true, as we all know.

A toast to Huang Ti, the greatest leader of all times!

It is not difficult to live a better lifestyle. What is hard is to overcome all the brainwashing and advertising which tries to persuade you to eat unhealthy foods, buy short-lived technology and follow fashions which are set-up simply to make money for someone else.

On the contrary, living a healthier lifestyle is pretty easy. Eat no meat, seriously avoid processed foods, too much sugar, fat and salt, smoking too, stop eating meat (and save money as well as health!), Then do some really simple but pleasurable exercise classes, like T'ai chi Chuan, around three times a week.

Humans have problems. Many humans have many problems. These problems vary but the basic weaknesses are the same. Overcome these, one by one, to reach the next level of development.

The Madness of the Human Race.

Taoism does have a well deserved place in today's society. Having had over two-thousand students pass through my Kwoon (Training Hall) Doors I have seen many who have had their lives changed for the better by studying and enjoying Taoist Arts, like T'ai Chi Ch'uan (Taijiquan), Kung-fu (Gongfu) or the other aspects. However, I have also seen too many, later distracted by western lifestyle, then becoming ill or imbalanced again, loosing all good they once had. This sticks in my mind. I had one man who joined one of my T'ai Chi & Ch'i Kung classes, an older man in his retirement years. He was ill. He had lost his wife and became so sad that grief made his lungs weak. He had just been diagnosed with cancer. Someone suggested my classes might help him, so he came along. He learned The Eight

Strands of Silk Brocade (qigong) and a simplified Taijiquan Form. Within six months he went for another check-up and was told that "mysteriously", the cancer had subsided and he was clear. His skin looked more natural and healthy and he had a more energetic air about him. After a year or so, he stopped coming. He had met another woman and desired female company, after all, he had been so used to it after 50 years. She persuaded him to go out on his training nights (only 2 per week out of 7!) so he went out instead. After another six months I saw him. He had stopped training at home and his Cancer looked like it was returning! I begged him to at least keep up the daily Eight Strands. He said he'd try. Within another year he was dead. He had stopped training, so the Cancer again preyed on his weak spots and killed him. The National Health Service were of no use whatsoever. All they could do was prescribe pain killers. Which course of action do you think he should have taken?

My Old Master also taught us about diet, lifestyle and some very basic but powerful healing techniques. These I have used many times to help people who were in need of being helped. You can read about some of the help and changes in my other books, T'ai Chi diet II – Ch'ang Ming. (Ch'ang Ming, by the way, means "Long Life", as in being helped by the Taoist Arts) and Qigong & Baduanjin (this introduces Qi or Ch'i and its concepts and realities.

So there we have it. An introduction into the philosophy of Tao and how it can be used wisely to improve the quality of living. The example above are using TCM because it not just about how we live. No. If we are pure, radiant and all good things you can imagine, it can still be a burden to us if all around us are ill, mentally unbalanced due to poor lifestyle and affecting everything which we do. This is why, in the very long history of Taoism, so many Taoists have helped others, at no cost, to get better. Alright, I say "no cost", but now we have to hire expensive halls to run classes in, so there may be some small cost, as such.

Grandmaster C. Chee Soo was in a five day a week job, but his evenings and weekend were given up to teach and help others. He was very popular due to his abilities to heal people. At one point, a grateful man he had helped, told him he could use his vacant shop on Edgware Road in London. The man man made him a sign to go over the door that said "Hoimar Brocade". There he spent a couple of evenings and time at weekends helping many people who had become ill. At the final count he had over 5,000 people on his list there, and he helped them all for free.

As an interesting side note: In olden days, a Chinese Doctor would hang a lantern outside his or her home for every life that he/she had saved. An interested person might then choose the doctor with the most lanterns, as they were potentially the best. The physician and patient would then sit down and talk, and a weekly fee agreed according to income. The Doctor would also find out as much about his new patient's health history, lifestyle, diet and working environment to get an idea of what the person might be like, health-wise or risk-wise.

(Image right: Dr Hua, T'o. Famous
Physician and creator of Acupuncture.)

If a patient became ill, then no payment would come in. The Doctor would then rush to see the patient at his or her home. If ill, then the physician would ask what changes there had been to diet, lifestyle or environment, then try to ascertain the cause correctly before applying any advice or help. The Doctor was committed to the patient and the prerogative was to keep the patient as healthy as possible so that the Doctor's income was not disrupted. Simple, yet effective.

Lao Tzu, Huang Ti and many others have left us a legacy of true value. They have left us valuable knowledge as to how we may speed up our educational processes, learning valuable Arts (high-level skills) that can change our lives, save our lives or even increase our spirituality. These are skills that governments of today do not want you to have, as they want to be in control of you, and make you weak and needy on their limited services.

The choices today are there, but you must chose wisely. Do you want the above, or do you want to live in an alien world where people are treated like fodder, encouraged to dull their minds and internal systems with strong drugs, processed foods, buy electronic gizmos that will enslave you, make you traceable and controllable in all you do. Is that freedom? Is that "good"?

CHAPTER THREE:

THE TAO OF YIN & YANG

To many a Western Scientist the items that are around us are separate and self-contained, or perhaps formed via a 'remote' chain of evolution. Everything is broken down into parts, each part is then labelled, broken down again and again until the item seems far removed from its original form. Molecules, protons, electrons and atoms are all treated as separate entities, almost as though they were not related or did not act in some form or other together! To the Taoist adept this shows a vulgar lack of understanding of the realities of Nature within the Universe. For he/she knows and understands that everything is indeed an interacting element with everything else. An old Taoist adage says, "the only thing which is predictable (constant) is change".

Non-definitive Definitions:

In order that we may more simply perceive the meaning of Tao, some basic graphic images were created which described the various aspects. Tao being the Ultimate, nameless form, means that these are not the definitive examples of what Tao is, merely parodies or analogies as to what happens within Tao.

Tao begins with nothing. Like the Big Bang theory, Taoists believe that there was Inaction, or Nothing, from this all creation emerged. The state of emptiness or nothing is called Wu Chi (Wuji) and is represented by a black sphere with an outer circle: the outer circle represents "within the Universe", while the black fill represents Yin, Chaos, Inactivity, non-active.

This graphic representation of theory, predates modern scientist's theory by hundreds, if not thousands of years.

Tao is the creation of life and movement which sprung forth from Wu Chi. The two major aspects or forces that occur in Nature (The Universe), those of positive & negative. These are termed in Chinese as ; Yin (Negative) , Yang (Positive) and are the most basic expressions of Tao.

In the simplest form they may be represented graphically as two triangles. Yang points downward, Monism. Yin points upward, Dualism.

(Fig: 1.)   ▼ Yang   ▲ Yin

To reflect these as a united, or combined force, they are superimposed on top of each other, Yang pointing downward, Yin pointing upward.

(Figure 2)   Dual-Monism.

Dual-monism represents the two basic forces of the Universe, up/down, dark/light, female/male, night/day, attract/repel, et cetera. The downward direction of Yang also represents 'outwards' and the energy of the universe is thought to flow out from the centre. As we stand on Earth and consider ourselves to be "upright" (even though we may be at any angle) we simply call it "downwards flow". This energy flows through the male body and into the earth (ground). The energy thin spins outward and "upwards" to return to the centre of the universe, or galaxy, again. On its way up it passes through the earth and formed the inverted female organs. Hence it is said that women get their ch'i with their feet firmly on the ground whilst men have their ch'i from the heavens; in theory, and very loosely, this says why men have "their heads in the heavens", meaning we like to explore and discover, whilst most women may have a more earthy quality and prefer parochial nest building; safe nest for babies.

Many people mistake this symbol for the one used by the Jewish culture which is almost the same but lacks the outer circle. As it is above though this symbol represents Tao. These symbols are often available as necklace jewellery throughout the western world. The same symbols may also be found in other cultures, outside of China.

Dual-Monism may refer to two forces of Nature, and they may also appear to be opposites, like man and woman. They are opposites but they are part of the same thing, so One. There is no separation in Tao, only harmony. You cannot have one thing without the other. Anyone who tries to create a rift or divide between one element and another has lost the proverbial plot. They are imbalanced and need to get back to unity again.

In many forms of animal nature these principles are echoed, to some degree, and the females show far better home building qualities than the male of the species who goes off either hunting or on exploratory trips. This does not always relate to the human animal as we can choose to go which way we like and can, within reason, change roles. Not that it always works out very well.

T'ai Chi literally translated means "Tao". The next symbol cleverly describes what happened after what we now call "The Big Bang". Tao went from passive mode to creative mode. Stars, planets, nebula and more were created and started to expand outwards, in a spiral action. This "spiraling" has been confirmed today by leading Space Scientists. Our planet spirals around the sun, the galaxy spirals, other galaxies spiral and they all spiral off into the great void.

(Fig: 3.)   The T'ai Chi.

Again Dual Monism is shown in this graphic. The two basic forces which rule everything are called Yin and Yang. Dual-Monism may

refer to two forces of Nature, and they may also appear to be opposites, like light and dark, active and inactive, man and woman. They are opposites but they are part of the same thing, One. There is no separation in Tao, only harmony. You cannot have one thing without the other. Anyone who tries to create a rift or divide between one element and another has lost the plot. They are imbalanced and need to get back to unity again.

More familiar to many thousands of people world-wide is the representation below. The two forces are still contained within the Universe, but this is usually made into a wider band. Yin is represented by the darker patch and Yang by the lighter patch. The basic pigments are used because they are opposites - light and dark. They are different but equal.

(Fig: 4.) Yin/Yang Tao.

Like a wheel it turns, for it flows constantly to represent the flow of nature's forces. Although the direction of flow can sometimes appear differently, sometimes by accident as the "artist" may not realise any particular significance. There are other translations according to belief, for example, some Taoist sects, schools or groups use different colours, blue and red, gold and silver, brown and blue, yellow and green. These still represent Yin and Yang, the two interacting powers of the Universe.

This image represents the constant flow of Yin forces and Yang forces, flowing throughout all things in the Universe. The symbol here depicts 'Harmony', for the two principles work together, like day and night, summer and winter, male and female, and rely on each other for 'Balance', neither one could exist in creation without the other. The "tear-drop" or "fish" shaped sections represent Yin (black) and Yang (white). Neither is superior, yet each may be more prominent at times. They are opposite qualities in phenomena, or principles: e.g. winter is Yin, but gives way to summer which is Yang, this in turn gives way to winter again and so the two work in harmony. If we use the term "forces" it is in the sense of the natural forces of the Universe. Yin and Yang both have the element of the other within them, signifying that neither is 100% pure but also that each needs the other at its core as without Yang Yin could not exist and vice-versa.

There is also the issue of gravity. Depending which side of the Equator you live, when water goes down a hole, or sink plughole, it will form a spiral, on one side of the Equator it is clockwise, on the other anti-clockwise. There is actually someone demonstrating this principle in a village on the Equator; you can discover that novelty for yourself.

The Force *is* With You.

After the separation and explanation of the Yin/Yang aspects, let us look at these two forces in more detail. Each has a different set of characteristics. Listed below are some of the distinctions given to them.

YIN	YANG
Chaos	Order
Negative	Positive
Dark	Light
Passive	Aggressive
Cold	Hot
Winter	Summer
Moon/Night	Sun/Day
Receiving	Giving
Wet	Dry
Soft	Hard
Stationary	Moving
Centrifugal	Centripetal
Expansive	Constrictive
Liquids	Solids
Lightness	Heaviness
Silence	Sounds.

Yang energy flows outward from the centre of Heaven (Centre of The Universe and/or Galaxy) whilst Yin is the returning energy. The ancient Taoist theory explains that the downward travelling force of

Yang coming through the male's body pulled the male sexual organs down and outwards. In the female the sexual organs were formed inwardly by the upward returning Yin forces as that returned from the Earth to the centre of "Heaven". This, at first seems amusing, but the theory seems to fit so perfectly with other aspects of life and account for basic tendencies which seem to be universal, so let us just take it as that, a basic difference formed by Nature and the forces of Yin/Yang.

As you can see from the above, partial list of "life things", having a knowledge of Yin and Yang can be an education by itself. You will also notice that certain 'elements' are featured. The most obvious of these are Water and Fire. There may be further distinctions in one thing, for example; A quiet sound is Yin, a loud sound is Yang by comparison.

Sometimes the above examples, when seen in such a list, may seem obvious. Understanding the interactivity of different elements in such a simple manner can add to our appreciation of nature and also serve to remind us of our relationships, or interrelationships. Each action that we make has an equal and opposite reaction. A loud noise leaves silence behind it, a loud argument between two people, one being forceful or shouting in temper, may leave the other withdrawn and quiet. It is best to avoid loud and aggressive people for they are not well developed in their natures and cause disruption to others by forcing their ill mannered and loud protestations on others.

Science has used many of these principles to aid invention, like "floating" a heavy and solid object on something soft and light; metal on a liquid oil bed, for example. That which is stationary controls moving things, like traffic lights, signs and roads control moving traffic. In Taijiquan (T'ai Chi Ch'uan) we use the mind to control the energy and body, so it is said that movement comes from within stillness. Another way of looking at that is when we sit still and quiet we often have our best ideas. These quiet spells lead to busy spells, so inaction leads to action, to move us forwards.

A Ship is a structure made from Yang/Metal, but is Yin/Hollow. It therefore floats on Yin/Water but can be sunk by Yang/Water!

When we have a very Hot and Sunny/Yang day, we often look forward to the cooler Yin/Night, with the sun's reflection off the Yin/Moon giving us reflected light. An educational book may also be thought of as "reflected light".

We can understand the interaction of the elements and we can also use them in problem solving, even if we are not called "scientists".

The effect of studying Tao is long term. It can take some months or years to alter the way that we perceive things or to put it another way, free our minds and open them so that awareness comes naturally, allowing us to see the true meaning of what happens around us.

In terms of Men and Women, these are dubbed Yang and Yin respectively. Regardless of petty politics nowadays (not necessarily a new thing!), men are men and women are women, but there will be many *variations* of Yang or Yin, some merging seamlessly into the other. This is also a subject area which you should study, the relationships of men and women, not just in human animals but in other animals too.

Generally speaking, both sexes are the same (human animal). Both men and women may even think in a similar way about any given subject, but there the similarity stops, or varies, at least. Bearing in mind that this is a generalisation and does not apply to all, men can be outgoing, aggressive, adventurous and inquisitive. Women can be more introvert and quieter, passive, stay-at-home and uninterested in whatever men may be inquisitive about. As stated above, this is a generalisation, as now, in the twenty-first century, there has been a women's movement and push to get more adventurous, compete with the men, or get involved in other pursuits that were seen traditionally as "male orientated"; and nothing wrong with that at all, it's just that "history" Usually written by political types) never used to accept women doing "men's things", but nevertheless they did; e.g. Amelia Earhart, Cleopatra, Helen of Troy, etcetera. This is where the lines appear to blur into grey, but still, do not be fooled, women and men are still the same but different! This is a very, very complex area, but here goes with an example. Politicians. Yes, sorry, but had to be done!

Women in general life use more subtle and shrewd ways, some can be even quite devious at times. This is a Yin quality as it is "indirect". When it comes to politicians, both female and male, they may also use the same Yin ways. This is not because of their sex but because of their mental state. Simply put, a person in balance will be part male, part female in their overall psyche: e.g. the subtlety is in which comes first. One Element balances out the other, so as Yang is stronger, if a male has more than 3 parts Yang, he may bee too aggressive. If a woman has too many Yin elements, then she may be too soft or too passive; imbalances in physical and mental health are all measured using a Yin/Yang scale.

Later in this book you will find the chapter on Chinese Zodiac. This has a description of a Lecture that I was invited to give to a group of western Astrologers. For this lecture and demonstration of the principles of Chinese Horoscopes I used four well known politicians at the time. The only well-balanced one was never elected as his personality did not come across as strong enough! The others were all imbalanced, therefore used louder, more persuasive and powerful ways to make themselves sound better; none were and they proved that by themselves!

When it comes to understanding Tao, Yin/Yang and Wu Hsing, my job is not to explain it all to you, but merely to open the door, let you see a glimpse of the path and then point the way.

THE TAO OF WU HSING

Tao can be further divided into not only the two major forces, but also the Five Major Elements (Wu Hsing, pronounced "Woo Xzing"). These are; Fire, Earth, Metal, Water and Wood. (AIR is taken to be a natural by-product of the other five, so is not included separately - a sharp observation indeed so many years back!). Each of these may be further categorised as being either Yin or Yang, depending upon their action at the time. Everything on the Earth and in Heaven is made up, in some form or another, of these elements. But the Wu Hsing are above all not literal translations of universal qualities but examples. By this it is meant, for example, that something may not necessarily be made of metal, but it may have the character of metal - for example a "Karate Chop" has the cleaving effect of metal, but as we know is done with flesh and bone. A knife is Positive Metal, because it has an active purpose, as does a spanner. A coin is Negative metal, it has no "active" function, a "token", and is therefore Yin. An argument may be Positive Fire, but if it is destructive then it can be Negative Fire. Something creative and constructive is Positive Wood (growth and expansion), whilst a wooden bowl is Negative, or Yin, as its purpose is to receive. The Elements and their interactions has to be studied.

There are far too many positive and negative instances in our everyday lives to go into here but this should suffice to give a few clues; a signpost to the path of enlightenment. Understanding such effects can have a subtle effect upon our lives as we come to appreciate, more and more, the results of our own actions in all that we do and use. Mahayana Buddhism comes close to this but I have never come across such a profound and deeply penetrating philosophy as Taoism. It is a psychologist's dream for there are so many areas of cause and effect to explore at so many levels.

It is a positive philosophy which can serve to describe things on a simplistic level, using graphic comparisons, call it a "lay science". On other levels it climbs the greatest heights and could be taught in schools from an early age, thus helping children to understand that all of their actions are like ripples in a pool, they spread out and touch others, cross over and even bounce back. Understanding the Wu Hsing properly can take years, but is worth it so persevere.

The illustration (Fig 5) below sets out the relationship of the Wu Hsing, the Five Elements. Each of these has a Yang nature and a Yin nature. Together they represent everything in known existence and even that of which we do not as yet know of.

(Fig: 5.)

TAO

|

Yin-&-Yang

|

Earth - Water - Metal - Wood - Fire

|| || || || || || || || || || || || || || ||

|||||||||| ALL THINGS IN EXISTENCE ||||||||

The elements have been arranged in the order above so that they fit, as nearly as possible, under the most appropriate position relating to their Yin/Yang status, i.e.; Fire = Extreme Yang and Earth extreme Yin, although each has a Yin or Yang side to its nature. In reality, the Universe has no 'order' or lists of what goes in first place or second, etcetera. A collision of two Yang objects may trigger and explosion, which is followed by minor Yang (spreading) and then by minor Yin (settling) and eventually Yin (still), but from this may come more new Yang, growth, as in the life of Nebula, where new stars and planets are born.

The diagram or symbol for the Wu Hsing, the Circle (Universe) containing both Yin and Yang triangles which connect with the Five Element points around the inside of the circle, showing interaction; I included the Yin-Yang symbol just to emphasise their Yin and Yang functions.

Wu Hsing

REGULATE or STIMULATE

Each of the five elements has times when it appears either negative (Yin) or positive (Yang). When this happens it usually interplays with some other element to perform some function (Yang) or as a result of some function or action (Yin). Let us look at some of the opposites - the Yin are Passive and the Yang are Active.

Yin:	Yang:
Electric Fire/Heat	Flames
Battery Energy	Explosion
Metal Coins	Knives
Metal Tray	Engine
Earth - soil	Rocks
Clay Pot	Wall
Window/Door Frame	Live Trees
Paper/Cardboard	Table

Pond of Water	Water Fall
Still Pond/Lake	Tidal Wave.

This use of passive and active also comes into TCM, Chinese Horoscopes and even T'ai Chi Ch'uan. There is much thought gone into all of these Sciences and Arts, over thousands of years. Each one, as you may begin to see, can have a valuable place in society; in any country; this may explain why the Taoist arts are always gaining in popularity.

My Thoughts.
How does this Philosophy relate to Psychology or even Sociology?

When your health is improving, you are in a Yang phase. When it declines you are in a Yin phase. In Traditional Chinese Medicine (TCM), these terms are used for Positive or Negative flow or effects.

In terms of Mental health, it is just the same. Many people in the world say they had a good day (Yang), then the next, a bad day (Yin). They are stating that the bad day had something wrong with it. It was not good, so it makes them feel remorse, sadness or to have misgivings. This is a very mild form of depression, so it is a mental health issue.

Psychology-wise, when we study Taoism, and learn these opposites, as in the lists above, we see that there are, always will be and always has been, opposites. Therefore, we learn and then train ourselves to accept that there will be good days and bad days, things which "go right" and others that "go wrong". This is just "life", or Tao, from a human perspective.

In terms of Sociology, we can see interactions here too. If someone lives in an area that is "nice", then someone comes along and starts smashing the place up, burglarising properties or bullying neighbours, then this is seen as the opposite to "nice", so is "nasty". That nastiness then casts a negative effect on the other residents who were once happy. They now feel sad, worried, depressed. In many cases, some of these affected people may themselves resort to unfair or foul actions. This then affects a wider area. What was once a "very pleasant housing estate" then become "a hell hole".

The issues here are clear. Those people who are causing problems have imbalances. If these can be dealt with, balance restored, then the problems might be "nipped in the bud". If the minor Yin phase is allowed to go unchecked, then it becomes a major Yin stage and causes all the negative effects. Many local Councils deal with "offenders" by providing Council housing on one estate, where the numbers of "offenders" grows, often creating crime and drug centres, gang areas, etc. If these people were instead offered an alternative to fines and imprisonment, such as a course on healthier eating (under strict guidance, maybe 'Residential'), then there is a chance that those who slipped off the path, may get back on it again and not be "offenders" thereafter.

Admittedly, this would take one heck of a lot of changes. We would need changes in Government at the top, local government, councils, support, and more, plus training in the first place for all those people who would be in the critical "driving seat" jobs, dealing with the offending clients. But imagine… imagine what differences it could make to society as a whole.

It can happen, I have seen it. People can be changed, not by force, but by influence, example and good leadership that sets good examples. I have seen it, perhaps you have too, but "Good News" is not often shown, whereas bad news travels fast! In the 1980's I witnessed CB Radio coming to UK. It literally transformed communities who became self-governing and ironed out problems without the need for police, courts or violence. This was later ruined by BT interacting with UK Gov over the loss of profits from Telephone Rental Bills.

Creation:

        The One begat two.
        The Two begat Wu Hsing,
        Ten Thousand Things Followed.

'Opposites' Verse.
To end this section a verse from some years back.

OPPOSITES (Yin/Yang)

Without the pain there'd be no pleasure

Without the night no lighter day

Without the work there'd be no leisure

And if no labour, then no play

Without the darkness there's no brightness

Without Autumn there'd be no Spring

My heart once heavy now filled with lightness

The silence pierced by birds that sing

Whilst meeting's joyful, parting's sorrow

Emptiness filled by arms that hold

Yesterday's memories not knowing tomorrow;

The sadness and the joys as yet untold.

Author: Myke Symonds. c.1991

CHAPTER FOUR:

Tao and Creation

Building on Chapter 3: The theory behind Tao and the creation of the Universe far pre-dates the modern scientists "Big Bang Theory" by at least 2,500 years. Taoist teachings, usually handed down by word of mouth, also use simple imagery over the centuries to tell the story like those in the previous chapter. Simple but profound graphics.

In the beginning there was space, usually seen as a void. There was no life, no action and no planets or stars. We may accept that there was some kind of "matter" in space, gases, atoms or elements which formed the basis for the so-called "Big Bang" as well as all things that followed. To simplify things Taoism uses the basics, thus starting with an empty void which is meant to represent the Universe before known existence. This nothingness was given the name of Wu Chi ("Wu-ji").

This image and idea is used at the beginning of the practice of Taijiquan, the practitioner emptying their mind and becoming still; this has a great calming effect and clears the mind for practice as well as having beneficial psychological effects, like remaining calm in the face of adversity, if practised regularly enough. Sometimes it is depicted as a white circle with a black edge. The outer circle depicts "within the Universe".

Chaos is sometimes associated with the state of the universe before Wu Chi, as chaos denotes disorganised arrays of many elements which had no purpose, function or interaction.

From Wu Chi sprang life and creation. The Universe erupted into life and created planets, and all other things that we know. This was achieved out of emptiness (described as Yin), by another force (Yang) or action.

Creation 'Jing'. The two forces spiraling out from the centre of the Universe represent Yin (black) and Yang (white) as they separate and become distinct identities and the Universe as we know it was created (Big Bang). These are the forces behind all things. This is a simple explanation and even peasants who could not read or write at the time could understand these images or ideograms. There are many thousands of things which are either Yin, Yang or a mixture of the two forces. As an example below are just a few easily remembered ones.

Opposite you see a photograph of a large Galaxy. This composes of spinning or spiraling objects which are Hard, like planets, rocks and other debris. Soft objects like Gasses, maybe even water droplets. Then we have hot or cold objects, like planets and moons, or Suns/Stars. Such a beautiful combination of Yin/Yang in its infinite formation, then it will change and re-form, carrying on for many millennia. This reminds me of a book I bought but never got around to reading; The Tao of Physics, by Fritjof Capra. In this book, he reflects on Physics, the power of the Universe, and uses analogy or likenesses from Chinese, Indian and other ancient cultures. There is a common school of thought among humans that other races, not from Earth, have visited and left behind symbols which reflect not only where they came from, but describing movements or orbits within our known

Universe as well. The Taoist Philosophy and images have been linked to a star body which we call Plaeidies, or "The Seven Sisters" group. Here is an edited photograph that I took of Plaeidies. The pattern of the Seven Stars, not to be confused with the Plough, are threaded throughout traditional Chinese culture. Is it possible that a race from that region visited China, mixed with the indigenous peoples and also left their knowledge of the Universe, complete with simple diagrams showing how the Universe works?

The forces of Tao Yin and Yang, The Eight Directions (Pa Kua or Bagua) and the Five Elements (Wu Hsing or Wuxing), in turn planets were created, stars, solar systems and of course from these sprang all manner of life. Patterns emerged, like day and night, summer and winter, male and female. The Pa Kua (Eight Major Directions), seen here, is often used to decorate Taoist halls, or courtyard areas. It is more than decoration though as students of The Way use this to contemplate different meanings and aspects of Tao – and therefore life. The Pa Kua is often used in exercises, like Taoist T'ai Chi /Yin -Yang Tao. They are contemplated and eventually trigger a realisation or action which signifies to the practitioner another step on their journey to enlightenment. Just as we study language, then mathematics and other subjects at school, Taoism is, what I call, a "Lay Science" and doubles as an educational Programme, which goes far beyond the basics and enters psychology, sociology and the spiritual realms of life too. It is the study of life, living and interaction with the world, and "Space", from a human viewpoint. The symbol that follows the spiral action of Jing is Yin/Yang-Tao, representing the constant flow of Yin and Yang, the main forcers within all things.

The Bagua or Pa Kua.

The **Eight Directions** represent not only the 4 main compass points plus the 4 in-between points, but in Taoist Philosophy are given reference points of things we know, such as Mountains, or the Sun.

The main meanings, in philosophical relationship, are these which connect with each of the Eight Trigrams: Heaven/Firmament - Tian, Wind - Feng, Fire - Huo, Mountain - Shan, Lake/Marsh - Zé, Water - Shui, Thunder - Léi, Ground - Dì (moving clockwise from the top Trigram).

Secondary they are describing the Five Elements, or Wu Hsing/Wuxing: Metal, Wood, Fire, Earth, Metal, Water, Wood Earth; but the repeats in different context.

The Pa Kua or Bagua then is used to describe the nature of Saintly people, animals, and much more. These images are used in Martial Arts training, Feng Shui (The Art of Divination) and even Traditional Chinese Medicine. More about these in following chapters.

Bagua and the Trigrams.

The Eight Directions are, as you can see by the Compass like illustration above, described by three lines, either solid or broken. These are called "Trigrams".

The image below illustrates just one Trigram, usually listed first as it is most important, for "heaven" created everything.

Chien/Qián/Heaven. The first Trigram, represents these things: the Creative, (natural) force, heaven, sky, northwest father, head-strong, persisting creative, and Horse.

As we can see, the symbolism used in Taoism is more sophisticated than just the Yin/Yang symbol, or the others described earlier.

This book is a general introduction to Taoism, not a complete Manual; that would take a lot more pages! The student of Tao, should you be and should you so wish, can perhaps "feel" where the proper pathway is to tread or follow. Perhaps you feel that you want to heal people? Then study proper, traditional Chinese Medicine (TCM) under a traditional teacher/practitioner. It is far more advanced than anything in the Western fields of medicine, especially as it tries to avoid toxic substances and anything unnatural.

Perhaps you feel a yearning in your Soul to learn the graceful Art of T'ai Chi Ch'uan/Taijiquan? Then again, find a traditional teacher who will also teach you Ch'i Kung/Qigong and perhaps even some TCM thrown in! Taijiquan should be far more than just learning a Form (Set of movements), and is not competitive in any way, let alone "going for gold". It is a lifestyle, linked with an age old philosophy which teaches you how to live a simpler, better and less complicated life.

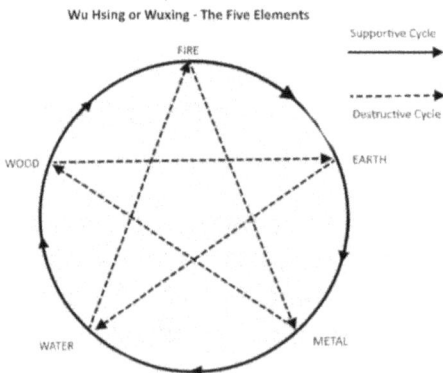

There are many fields of study that you could enter into, including the above, or Feng Shui, etcetera, but it has to be what is *in your heart*.

The Five Elements or Wu Hsing. The Five Elements are: Fire – Earth – Metal – Water - Wood.

They are noted here in their "creative cycle" and in relationship to mankind, the Human Animal. Fire is at the top because this represents the Human Mind, thinking, discovery and active processes.

The Cycle: fire induces earth, earth induces metal, metal induces water, water induces wood and wood creates fire. The creative cycle follows the outer circle in a clockwise direction.

In their "destructive cycle", flowing from point-to-point, fire controls metal, metal controls wood, wood controls earth, earth controls water and water controls fire. The controlling or "destructive" cycle follows from Fire, diagonally down to Metal – at the 5 o'clock position – then continues to Wood, Earth, across to Water and back to Fire.

This "relationship" is used in Chinese Astrology and Chinese Medicine, such as Acupuncture: the "Elements" are symbolic of the effects that one diseased organ or function can have on another.

In Psychology, the Fire (emotions) can sometimes be out of control, therefore "Wood" needs to be reduced and "Water" used correctly to control the "flames", so to speak. Being over-creative, or over thinking, can induce a psychologically imbalanced state. Water in this case refers to "stillness", like a small lake or a calm pond. Have you ever noticed that when you sit by a lake or a pond that your mind becomes still or more relaxed? Meditation is stillness, so is regarded as being like still water. Placid. As in all things, we need to have balance; balance = harmony, peace, equilibrium (the Motto of T'ien Ti Tao P'ai.) The controlling factor is Fire below Water.

From the Five Elements, we get the "Ten Thousand Things". Bear in mind that in ancient China, or elsewhere several thousand years ago, "10,000" was a huge number to imagine, let alone instantly name Ten thousand Things! Let us suffice to say that this clever yet very simple philosophy can be used to name just about anything by associating it with any of the Five Elements and their Yin/Yang variants.

Look at a tree. Wood, right? But the fact that the tree has roots that push down and into the ground makes them Yang. Their function is to channel water, which is Yin. They also cleave or split the soil, which is a Yang trait of Metal or Wood. The roots are reflected at the other end by branches which spread (Yang) and leaves which then gather sunlight (Yin) to use as energy for growth (Yang). The tree produces blossom (Yang) and fruit (Yin) which then fall to the ground. The Sun is yang (hot/bright), but it warms in a passive way. If you meditate long enough you can find more Yin/Yang actions. One of my all time favourite meditations, and life enhancing, is to think about one thing in Nature, then follow it through, from birth to death, to rebirth, with all of its interactions with other elements.

Take a coin from your pocket. Is it Metal? Is it Yin or Yang?
A pair of scissors. Metal. Are they Yin or Yang?

A house. How many Yin/Yang things can you find in the building?

The Ten Thousand Things.

The Ten Thousand Things table can be used to analyse and describe many things. Perhaps one of the greatest uses has been in Traditional Chinese Medicine (TCM). By diagnosis, observation and then labelling each element, a TCM Doctor can understand which parts of the system or body are out of balance. Then, by comparing that to what the balance should be, can start to see what is is wrong and what is needed to *restore* the balance.

TAO
|
Yin/Yang
| |
Wu Hsing
| | | | |
"Ten thousand things"
| | | | | | | | | | | | | | | | | | | | | | | | | | | | | | | | | | | | | | | | | | | |

In terms of psychology and sociology, a trained observer can establish why the person or the situation, perhaps a whole housing area, is off-balanced. This alone could include many of "The Ten thousand Things"", such as foodstuffs and their Yin/Yang state, surroundings, any chemical or other influences, *lifestyle addictions** or even "Social Status" (a purely imagined condition!)

Lifestyle Addictions include the way that certain people *expect* to be seen, or think that they *have* to be, because of where they were brought up or other conditions which become engrained in the locale or close society; e.g. someone brought up on a poor council estate may think they have to take basic jobs, or are not worthy of higher status, because this has been ingrained into the views of society. It is nonsense, of course. You can be whomsoever you want to be, or feel you should be, a basic worker, industrial leader or even President. Some people are born into rich families and are conditioned to think that they are supreme, elite or born leaders. Nonsense of course. The world is seeing at present (2022) some self-proclaimed 'Leaders' who are mentally imbalanced, destructive, self-serving and downright arrogant. They think they are normal but their actions paint a different picture. Normality suggests balance, and balance suggests harmony. A "Normal" person would not seek to kill 59,000,000 people,no matter how much resources they used up! Psychologists may label such people as "Sociopathic".

Imbalanced leaders try to control one situation by introducing new measures to contain it by force or by laws. This is like trying to put a small sticking plaster on a hole in a ship's hull, the pressure of the larger ocean will make the sticking plaster give way in the end. The answer is to discover the weak points, then build a stronger hull, or support structure. At that point. In society this translates as better education, better Natural diet, more pleasant housing conditions, work opportunity, tearing down old Social Classes and building the idea of public teamwork. We are all part of the same great community, each community is a part of the country, each country a part of the same planet. Harmonise, not separate.

Once you have discovered what the Ten thousand Things are, then you can take any item, situation or function and trace it back. Where does that go? Tao.

The original name was not "Ten Thousand Things", but the saying that OF 万物 WHICH MEANS "ALL CREATED THINGS". IN ORIGINAL TAOIST TEACHINGS THEY SAY THAT THE ONE (TAO) BEGAT TWO, TWO BEGAT ALL THINGS. (CHINESE: 道生一， 一生二， 二生三， 三生万物)

This is why Tao is impossible to name. How can you name something so enormous, so variable with so may millions and trillions of elements, especially those that are constantly changing? Therefore, Tao – The Way, substitutes all other descriptions and gives us something that we can then comprehend means "Life The Universe and Everything"!

That phrase above comes from a delightful story, which I gleefully preserve here. Douglas Adams, author of the 'Hitch-hiker's Guide to The Galaxy' series, was at Cambridge University. He needed a new computer for his writing. At the local shop, circa 1980's, was shown an Amstrad Word Processor PC. Allegedly, Adams asked the salesman, "What can it do?" The salesman replied "Just about anything. A computer can work out just about any equation that you give it!" When Adams got home, he set it up and when he turned it on, a little Cursor blinked in the bottom left corner of the Monitor. He had not yet inserted the Disk Operating System. So he thought he would challenge the new Personal Computer's "brain power". He typed, "Life, the Universe and everything?" The prompt answer came back "42".

Irony or what? Some years later, Astrophysicists stated that mathematically, "42" was a very important and often recurring number in the Universe! Could it be that your Computer knows way more than it is letting on?

In Taoism the number 8 is a very special number too. It is also considered lucky, but I am not sure of that. I had a car with a number "8" on the registration plate. It was hit in the rear several times. My youngest, Ray, just ten at the time said "Perhaps 8 is only lucky in China Dad?!"

Those of you who have studied Mathematics and/or Numerology, may realise the significance of numbers. There appears to be something more to it than just labelling items '1', '2' or '3'.

Feng Shui – the Art of Divination – can also use numbers, very effectively. The basics relate to the Taoist philosophy, the Eight Directions and your date of birth. Beyond that, I know little of the subject as it is a Specialist subject.

There was one story I read of a Feng Shui Master in Hong Kong. He was called in to look at a failing business. The Staff, mainly Chinese, were worried that they may loose their jobs, so begged the boss to call in the Feng Shui Master. He came, had a good look at the facade of the building, the layout inside and asked questions about the founder and when the business was set-up, etcetera. He went away, drew up some plans and the business was then shut down while builders moved the Front Door, Reception Desk and made a few other alterations, according to the Feng Shui plans. The business reopened. Within a few months trade had picked up, profits overtook losses and it was a success.

People who do not know, or have no experience, may scoff at such things. Having had some experience myself, I do not scoff, but believe that there is something in it. Having used basic Feng Shui myself, it changed my life and brought me to a new location, which (out of my personal control) happened to be the right layout and directions for me. Thank you Tao.

The Eight Directions or Pa Kua, are also symbols of family, actions, function or direction, such as South (Chien) = Heaven, Sun, 'Peng' control. It represents the force of Heaven creating order by control.

Kun, represents North (Kun) = Earth, 'Lui' receive. It represents the ability to receive and regenerate the creative energy. (Solid lines represent Yang, whilst "broken" lines represent Yin. These symbols are called Trigrams and each have a representation of functions, and are made up of three lines each and comprise a set of 8 x 8 = 64 in total.

Trigrams can be paired to form a Hexagram (six lines). Here we see a combination of Chien on top and Kun below, this is called P'i and translates as "Stagnation". The Yang is above the Yin, thus controlling it. This creates a situation where the two forces are at an impasse, stagnant. Nothing productive can be achieved. If Kun was on top, this would form T'ai "Prospering", bringing peace as Yin is dominant.

Are They Just Symbols?
When you look at the Hexagrams, you can see that it is just two basic images, a unbroken line or a broken line. These are used in different formulas, as Trigrams, which can then be put one on top of the other to make a Hexagram. These are symbols. Humans use symbols as directions or clues. These are clues as to Universal releationships.

63

Trigrams, Hexagrams and The I-Ching.

There is another Taoist works which is very well known, and used. This is called 'I-Ching' ("Yee jing"), which means "Book of Changes". This is a totally unexplainable book, original author unknown, which is used for what they generally call "divination" (telling the future"). Sounds crazy? Read on.

Most readers who are interested in Psychology will, of course, have studied at least some of the thoughts of Carl Jung (the most famous student of Sigmund Freud.). He had a Chinese friend who had a copy of the I-Ching (Book of Changes). Jung saw him consulting the book one day and challenged him. The friend told him that the I-Ching was intelligent, and that it could connect to the Universe and help to find answers to problems when one was really stuck or perplexed. Jung said that was nonsense, and the book was just cleverly written by a master of grammar to fool you into thinking it was correct! His friend let him have the book to examine. Jung then read, re-read, studied the chapters hard and tried to decipher what he thought was "the author's clever plot too fool people with words"! He even used the , what they call, "divination technique" of using small sticks or twigs, or a set of three clean coins.

After a couple of months, he took the book back. He admitted to his friend that each chapter was entirely different in content, so there could be no way that so many "random castings" of Sticks or Coins could come up consistently with answers that suited the problems! He even admitted that he had "asked the book" about an issue he had been trying to resolve in his own mind, but simply could not find the right answer. The book did! Carl G. Jung then ended up with his own copy of the I-Ching and used it frequently to obtain an unbiased and sensible answer to questions.

After a discussion about this one day, I myself decided to see whether or not the book could be fooled. After getting my copy out, kept in Black Cotton cloth, cover facing northwards) I asked it a irrelevant question about something I had made up. The Hexagram which came back as the answer, had no Moving Lines, so was just one very short verse in response. In so many words it said, "If you have nothing better to do than waste time, then get on with those things you have left undone."! That was me told!

It is inexplicable as to just how this humble book connects with the Universe and the owner's life and events.

The object of this book is not only to explain something of the Philosophy of Tao, but to show the many connections. The author has spent many decades studying these things, so it would be impossible to compress all thoughts, experiences and conclusions between these covers. Instead, you are left to look at the proverbial "Signposts" and then walk in the direction which you feel is your "Path". This means some readers may take a broader view and study many things along the way. Others may feel the urge to walk the pathway of psychology, or sociology, with a view to working in mental healthcare or perhaps social environmental planning, education or other forms. Some may study T'ai Chi Ch'uan, hence developing their own energy and spirit, growing more in-tune with Tao both as an individual and perhaps even as a Teacher.

My life's work has been mapped out for me. From four or five years of age I was studying Nature, practicing T'ai Chi Ch'uan (although myself or nobody else had an inkling what it was back then, in the "dark ages" of no TV, books or knowledge in the family!) Plus my distinctive style of sorting out two bullies on the first day of Infant School kind of gave the game away, had anybody have known the "style"! Spirit Guides of all sorts, being "lead" from one discovery to the next, one teacher to the next, were all inescapable events for me. To others, I guess I was just "that different boy", and still am. If you had my life, my experiences, then all I can say is that you would have no doubt whatsoever about the mysterious hidden powers of the Universe and how life is mapped out for most of us on this little planet.

Studies, as mentioned herein, have included many years of Psychology; but on a "free scale", not a limited set course. Sociology; well, all you need to do is "people watch", then find out more about diet, lifestyles and applied social grouping, etcetera, and it comes quite easily over time.

Problems.

Problems arise where planning goes awry and events are not as predicted or expected. From my viewpoint, I have seen far more problems arise from those who have been on College or University courses studying these subjects. Why? Is it because the courses are so short? Is it because the course organiser was prejudice, had to cut corners, save time, or make alterations to please a senior who was not perhaps "on the same wavelength"? Quite possibly one or even all three or more; bad planning, lack of time to follow through, lack of constant involvement, infrequent client contact and long waiting lists, etcetera. Beware those on courses!

During my teens I met those who were at University and studying such courses. Some talked complicated twaddle, just using big words but not threading them into the conversation to make a strong fabric, instead leaving big holes! Some of these I nicknamed "The Clock face Conversation", because they seem to have Twelve big words, sixty smaller ones, and filled the seconds with common words; I doubt 3600 though. All these things caught my attention and puzzled me, so giving plenty to meditate on and study. This kind of "life study" I would highly recommend more of, and more highly than the average "set" or "limited" coursework.

Life is a varied thing, as you already know, otherwise you would not have had your curiosity stirred. Intelligence is varied too, a multi-level, multi-faceted thing which cannot be easily marked out with a grid, one-to-a-thousand levels, or given convenient tags or labels. Intelligence is a very illusive and very grey area. You may already know this, but if you do not, then you will notice as years roll by. This is why I like the Taoist Philosophy as it treats all people as part of Tao, Tao's creation, be they Yin, Yang, Negative Water, Positive Wood or whatever? Yes, we use labels like those, but labels that are so popular in the western world now, like Bi-Polar, OCD, ACD and many others, I feel can be destructive; especially if treated with drugs; and many drugs are simply "experimental"! To me, someone called Autistic is just another human, another seed of Tao. There have been times when I have had far more intelligent, observational or humorous conversations with "labelled" people than with those who think they are normal or superior.

Try to be open-minded. Tao is.

As you may have already noticed, I like to mention books that I find useful as I type and in context, not Bibliographically. Therefore:

The Tao of Power, by R. L. Wing. (A 'I-Ching' translation.)

The Oracle of Change - Alfred Douglas (Penguin) and my personal choice, although the other one is pretty good and useful too.

Practical Philosophy of Tao - Myke Symonds - Life Force Publishing. A book which was intended mainly for schools or anyone who may be studying Tao or Taoism and wants a graphic rich description of the practical side of the philosophy with history and useful detail.

The Way of Life - by Witter Bynner.

The best translation of the original Chinese Bamboo scripts, studied by Dr Kiang (a traditional Chinese "poetic" language expert) and then passed to Mr Bynner for his English poetic skills. Very clear and without the too often found "intellectualism".

It worries me today when I see young people, even children as young as 5, playing electronic games, which are designed to be addictive, yet teach us nothing of any value. When I see a house with no books in it, that is even more of a worry.

Books represent years and years of study and accumulated knowledge. To read a book such as philosophical debate is an absolute privilege. To learn about Life is a greater privilege, but to learn about health, natural medicine and diet, or how to have a positive effect on people's lives, holistically, through training, is a truly valuable gift.

CHAPTER FIVE:

INTERACTION OF TAO IN NATURE

In this chapter we will look at a few interactions, from people to the world around us, and see how they sit within the philosophical concepts.

The obvious examples of the interaction of Tao in Nature must surely start with the most commonly seen fluxes of Yin and Yang. Every morning we stretch and open our eyes to a brand new, unique day. The day is Yang and interchanges constantly with night (Yin) and so the two flux and flow, as long as the Sun (Yang) shines. There is much more to our days than just this though.

Winter is Yin, cold, dark and stagnant (growth-wise). Summer is Yang, warm, light and progressive (growth-wise). These two elements also flow in turn. But there are also lesser, or new Yin (Autumn) and lesser or new Yang (Spring), etcetera.

YIN	YANG
Winter	Summer
Autumn	Spring
Night	Day
Evening	Dawning

Autumn is considered Lesser Yin, whilst Spring is Lesser Yang. This can also apply to evening 'Dusk' or morning 'Dawn' as well.

Now that we have large Optical, Digital and Radio telescopes in Space, we are discovering more and more about this vast cosmos that we live in; we tiny, tiny creatures, on one tiny planet, amongst a vast ocean of other suns and millions of other planets.

The Taoist theory about the creation of the Universes, which has been used for hundreds of years, starts with Chaos: uncreative gases and atoms, minerals and all sorts, just floating around in a mega-vast sea of emptiness. Then the so-called "Big Bang" happened, atoms collided, gasses exploded, and action was begun. Since then, gigantic gas clouds exploded and sucked in minerals and other matter, to form new stars and new planets in what we call "Nebula". The nearest that you can see, with a decent telescope or binoculars, is the Orion Nebula. Beyond that we have literally thousands of Galaxies. Some are like our own, the 'Milky Way', whilst others are still forming or crashing together to form new formations. How this merger affects life on planets we do not know, yet. Space is not, well... space. It is not really empty. It is full of gasses, energies and other matter or elements that are all still floating around, or like Comets, hurtling around at phenomenal speeds. On our tiny planet, we have similar natural occurrences in the form of earthquakes, volcanoes, Teutonic plate shifts, all happening spontaneously. Nature did not plan them. Nor can we plan for them not to happen. This is the broader spectrum of Tao which we can see at present. In the not so distant future, there may well be a few more surprise discoveries in store; in fact, I would bet on it.

As human animals on this tiny planet we should be learning how to live in harmony with it. Not mass producing "plastic junk" on such a scale that it chokes the planet's landfill, waterways and seas. By allowing politicians to rape countries of their minerals such as Lithium (Afghanistan, mainly), then build and sell electric cars for example, or create chemical plants which make unnatural substances, toxic drugs, unreal foodstuffs, etcetera, we are being negligent.

Everyone, not just the few, should be looking towards natural foods, natural heating, or at least low cost and cheap, if not free, to everyone: Nicola Tesla did this, as he somehow discovered the secret to making Free Energy. But he died *mysteriously* of a heart attack and the FBI raided his house and took all his files and plans. Now someone called Musk and others are somehow investing billions every year into building Tesla's inventions and selling them for huge profits; all except Free power, or Free Anything, completely against Tesla's plan! This is not Tao, this is the *greed* and unthinking result of it within our species. This kind of "pull up the ladder Jack" thinking needs to go, if we are ever going to survive and develop.

The ancient Taoists saw this coming. They devised a simple strategy to observe Nature, including Human Nature, then through their observations, create templates of philosophical and moral, health and better ways of living; and not just "living", but living together, for we all have to share whatever resources there are on this planet. These are running out fast, mainly due to overpopulation; that subject has already been breeched, so ladies, you are in charge of reducing the Earth's ravaging.

Living naturally is becoming harder and harder to do. Because there are an overabundance of humans on the planet, more food is needed. This makes suppliers use methods to force grow or by using chemicals or other treatments to make food grown faster or out of season. Because there are so many supplies of vegetables being grown, insects that feed on them also produce more, for there is an abundance of food for them to rear babies on. Animals thrive when the living is easy, but breed less when it is not. This means that the rising population in humans causes the rising population in insects that like our foodstuffs. Farmers therefore create new ways of killing off these bugs that eat crops meant for us, so that is why pesticides have been invented and used so widely. This really is a "vicious cycle"!

How Can We Change?
Ch'ang Ming is a good place to start. Ch'ang Ming means "long life", but is usually associated with the Natural diet that Taoists have studied, developed and propagated for many centuries now. You can read more about that in the 'Tao of Food' section. By changing the way we eat, we change the planet. Part of the food chain problem we have now is foods being grown out of season, or being shipped half-way around the world in jet aircraft or in deep-freeze containers on a ship; both craft emit polluting fumes too. The Human Animal is not really any different to most other animals on the planet. If there is an abundance of food, then the survival instinct will kick in and say "Eat, quick, before it all goes!" That natural instinct has ben around since cave man days, when food was not always abundant. Animals build up an instinct to eat what they can when they do not know where their next meal is coming from. We do though. It's just down the road in a convenient Supermarket, all we have to do to "forage" nowadays is get in the car, or on the bus, go to the shops and get as much food as we can carry. And we can be picky! To change the planet for the better, all we have to do is eat when hungry, eat for nutrition and health, and then eat more localised produce. Sounds easy, eh?

This is Taoism and Sociology. By studying better ways to live, being less greedy, less selfish, we can all pull together and, literally, change the world. Humans do need to control breeding though!

The Tao of Psychology is something which connects with the Tao of Sociology. Every human needs to know the facts, as stated above. We all need to understand our lifestyle, habits, what makes us eat more or what makes us live longer. Then we can work on ourselves. It is only if we work on our own body, mind and soul, can we hope to influence our children or our friends. The philosophy of Tao helps us to understand 'life', as we call it. To put all the pieces of the puzzle down in front of us so that we can study and connect them, in order to make full picture. Only when we look at the greater picture can we start to appreciate small details.

TAO
|
Heaven
|
Earth
|
All Life & Growth
|
The Human Animal
|
All Other Animals

Study that diagram from the top down (creation), then the bottom upwards (relation). Meditate on the connections and effects.

Everything is connected. Yet some humans seem to think that they stand alone in life, or even in the Universe. Why? Is it because those people who have learned to study Business, Economics and Politics at University have also learned how to use Marketing, TV and Social Media as a weapon of choice? Are we so brainwashed that we really believe that we need a whole "barrow load of [crafty] monkeys" to tell us what to do, what to eat, how to live?

In the west we have had many a great philosopher, yet many ignore them for the elaborate works of poets or psychologists who twist words and brains with fanciful language. One of the greatest, in my opinion, was Edmund Burke (1730 - 1797), born in Dublin, Ireland, January 12th 1729 or 1730. He was the son of a Solicitor. Being a great thinker, and observationalist, he was known briefly as a philosopher, but his later involvements lead him to study politicians (rather than politics), for whom he had great contempt, so it would seem. Rather than me running into many quotes, I suggest that you, dear reader, look this fine man up for yourself and enjoy his witty, but "tongue in cheek" critique born from his observations. Suffice it to say, the man seemed to think that politicians were unfit to rule the working people, let alone understand the higher realms of philosophy.

Think about it. Who shapes the world we live in? Of course, the Politicians, not philosophers (If only!) Just imagine what would happen if your government Politician debates were replaced with just 10% Philosophers. You would hear the usual childish jibes, sarcastic remarks and often character assassinating acidic comments, interspersed with the odd, "May I remind the honourable gentleman that his remarks are out of sync with the way of life. We cannot put a sticky plaster on a thousand-year-old mummified corpse and expect it to gain immaculate function. We need to start afresh!"

After studying those in positions who considered themselves "elite", Burke proffered this advice to his friends and colleagues:

> "First, That all jurisdictions which furnish more matter of expense, more temptation to oppression, or more means and instruments of corrupt influence, than advantage to justice or political administration, ought be abolished.
>
> Second, That all public estates which are more subservient to the purposes of vexing, overawing, and influencing those who hold under them, and to the expense of perception and management than of benefit to the revenue, ought, upon every principle both of revenue and of freedom, to be disposed of."

Quite clearly what he was suggesting here is that there was a tendency toward corruption and self-serving power. Has anything changed since the 1700's? It seems not. Those who seek power will seek positions from which they can exude that power with authority as their shield. Meanwhile, philosophers and wise men look an and only make public comment, which the majority never get to hear of, such as Burke's assessment of the situation in which corrupt men, and women. Seek to use politics (ruling the working classes) as a tool to oppress and destroy while lining their own nests. They, in their Yin state, poison the minds of the masses and rape the world of its resources. Then they blame the general populace.

> "All that is necessary for evil to succeed is for good men to do nothing, as they must if they believe they can do nothing. There is nothing worse because the council of despair is declaration of irresponsibility; it is Pilate washing his hands." *Edmund Burke*

Pilate, of course, just in case any reader is unaware, Pilate authorized both the flogging and crucifixion of Jesus. This was *after* he had earlier announced that he could not see that the man had done anything wrong; but then conceded to political pressure.

This is the madness of power and what happens when men or women stray way off the path and seek only selfish ends. On the contrary, those who study philosophy usually find sanity, understanding and inner peace. However, the Philosophy of Tao is not just about one person, or one Mind. Tao concerns every aspect of life, or as I like to call it, "Life, The Universe and Everything."

When we think about the interactions of Tao in Nature - Nature being what I call "the footprint of Tao" - it is a generalisation which includes humans, other animals, plants, mountains, Space, planets and stars, etcetera. This is what makes the Taoist philosophy stand out from the crowd... not that there is a "crowd" when it comes to philosophy schools. It may well explain why Taoism is the most popular philosophy study in the world today. Though it must be noted here that not many people shout "hey! I'm a Taoist." As much as they do proclaim to be a Buddhist, Muslim, Jew or a Christian, for example.

These Words Are Mine.
No. These words are not mine, I just found them in the dictionary and put them all together in this order after thinking.

This little book is not about making a profound statement, or saying that "this is the way we must…". This little book is about TAO, but also how the Practical Philosophy of Tao ties in with Psychology and Sociology. Despite being three separate courses in a university, or three separate books on a shelf, these three subjects are, in fact, as inseparable as all things under Tao. This book, along with my own thoughts and interlinked observations, is about having the personal power and potential of changing the quality of Life.

MY FOUR SEASONS

A change of pace and style. A slightly poetic observational trip through some of the more 'obvious' parts of the seasons as I see them.

SPRING: (New Yang)

Throughout this season we can see the most conspicuous changes occur. There is the Dawning of New, the budding of trees and the blossoming of flowers, buzzing of the bees. Sunshine and showers mingle with the busy breeding of creatures great and small, they chirp and they chatter with bright mating call. The air is filled with vibrant morning mists and the earth seems to stretch and yawn after what can seem a long hibernation period. The sleepy trees stretch out their branches to capture the light and lovers take notice and go out at night. This is the season of Spring. And I bet it is probably your favourite time of year, a time to rejoice, for renewal is here!

SUMMER: (Yang)

Summer brings out the fledglings, finding their wings and the blossoms on the trees and outstretching leaves. Then rich green leaves and grasses sway in balmy breezes, sometimes hazy blue skies and hard working farmers toiling and tilling and thing and frying. Oh, the sweet perfume of of Summer flowers fills up the air. Bird's song is echoed around the treetops and the countryside lays out a fresh green carpet to herald the coming of the light. Out come the hampers, the cameras, too, as people rejoice and find things not to do. The small town gardens burst forth with their secluded blossoms. In Summer our hearts are filled with joy and the desire to be closer to Mother Nature's warmth and nurturing.

AUTUMN/FALL: (New Yin)

As the air begins to chill, the leaves die off in blazes of gold and reds. The squirrels store their larders of Autumnal fruits and eat their fill. Whilst children become excited at the prospect of Bonfire Night and baked potatoes, fireworks and family frivolity. The fields are ploughed to air the soil and cleave the way for next year's crop and more Farmer's toil. The birds chatter in the trees before going swiftly home to sleep, "Where did you go today? What did you find to eat?". Autumn is the time when we sit and remember the things we liked about the Summer gone. Some regret that they never got around to doing all they favoured. The home fires light and curtains drawn, we quietly sit and withdraw from too much outdoor activity, dose quietly and dream of things that we liked. Laying on sunny banks, catching "tiddlers" in the dike. The carpet of gold crunches under our feet as the trees recycle their nourishment so that the soil can eat.

WINTER: (Yin)

Winter steals in, like a thief in the night, its steel-cold claws rape the Sun's pale lemon warmth. It is time to stay in, or gather around the Public House fire, to chat and watch the long evening expire. The scavenging Crows take corpse from the road and Hares dart around in Winter abode. When snows come, as often they do, the revelling children in scarves make for fun. Blackbird and Thrush pick the last Winter berries. As we struggle with shopping in cold, cutting winds, we think of the Spring, from whence new cycles begin. At the end of the season, the long cold nights tell, summer's tale heralds well we see expectant mum's with proud belly swell!

The TAO of Interaction in Nature

One of my favourite places, just south of Norwich, overlooks some of the best scenery in Norfolk. Being a high spot, you can see for miles around. There you can see rolling hill and dale (Yin/Earth), trees (Yang/Wood), roads (Yang/Earth) and railway track (Yin/Metal). No matter which way the wind is blowing, it always seems to be coming from the South-West! The clouds (Yin/Water) drift by like sailing ships driven by the perpetual, swirling air currents (Yang) and Mother Nature in her fullest may be observed quiescently from this wonderful viewpoint atop the small hill behind old Caistor St. Edmund's Old Hall.

The various "going's on" and the scenery itself make for an interesting tapestry of life, fluxing with the the Tao, Yin, Yang and the Wu Hsing (Five Elements). Possibly the most notable force to the observer is the wind or breeze. It rustles the leaves on the trees, sways the tall grasses and crops, whispers around your ears incessantly and fans you on a summer's day. The wind (air) is just a by-product of the other elements, the heat and cold producing pressure fronts which displace (Yang) or attract (Yin) the air. Warm air makes the water evaporate and rise (clouds) while cold air (Yin) makes it rain or snow.

From there, on the hill, one can look at the trees of many varieties and see, passionately to the core, the roots and below, the leaves and above. Here the element of water, carried in the clouds, rains down upon the soil and is soaked away (Yin). Not all is returned to the babbling brooks and rivers though. The roots of the steadfast trees take their rightful share of water. This promotes the growth of the wood element - crops and other vegetation also are 'wood' element - and the action of growth is positive, or Yang. The Rain coming down is Yang whilst the soaking away is Yin. Together they work and the trees can absorb the Carbon gasses which are harmful to us and produce oxygen which is beneficial to Humans and other species of animals.

From the distance one can hear the rumble of the Inter City train coming from London and Ipswich to Norwich. The metal tracks carry the speeding engine (Yang) as the passengers sit and think of shopping or home comforts. Nowadays the trains are electric (Fire) and are powered from overhead lines. Even larger Electricity Pylons can be seen looming over the distant landscape and clashing with Nature's softer view. These huge, passive (Yin) metal pointed towers (Yang) carry the moving energy (Yang) to feed the power hungry applications of home and industry (Yin). These features and more can be seen on the narrow lane by which one sits as cars growl by, their engines straining as gears are changed and their drivers scurry like auto-mobile mice from a-to-b. On a sunny day the (Yang) rays of heat and light from the sun warm the skin and the cool (Yin) air from the breeze is refreshing.

Martine comes by on her horse 'Bells', as she hacks her way around the scenic paths. Here again there is a constant interaction between horse and rider, one guiding and one reacting. But every so often the horse makes its own presence and will known, then the rider has to listen and interpret, then respond to the horse!

All around in Summer are the growth (Yang/Wood) of crops and plants. Beside the seat on which one sits (Yin/Wood) are Poppies, tall and short silky grasses, nettles and more. Each of these spreads its seeds which lay dormant until the following year. Not all is dormant (Yin) during the Winter . There are still the Evergreen trees, the Winter Barley, Cabbage and such. Other activities also continue and some even flourish on the Yin quarters. During the Summer (Yang) there are many fruits that are borne and many creatures that eat their fill and sleep it off. There are lots of other Yin things happening, like the storing of food and the shedding of coats. During the late Summer there is the rotting and decay (Yin) of matter to produce richer soil (Yin) with which another years harvest may flourish.

So much goes on before our very eyes, but the average person is so preoccupied with those daily chores and worries that it all goes by unnoticed. Such is the pace of some people's lives that they slave and worry every day, always trying to earn more money tokens for bigger and better possessions, only to find that they either have a heart attack or that by the time they retire they are so restless that they cannot relax and enjoy retirement. Some folk even find that their golden nest-egg is snatched away by yet another unscrupulous business or government plan. What is the point? As they say, you cannot take it with you. Your life can be enriched and you can 'see' yourself and others more clearly by studying the Tao. In the essential arts of living, there is no point in doing futile things or things which make you feel worse or which have to be "hidden" behind veils of excuses.

It would be far better if all try to live with an understanding of the Way of Nature and then there will be better health and better harmony. Yes, there are predators and prey, growth and destruction, life and death in Nature. But is all of the natural variety, not some government scheme or business plan. Those that kill do so for food, although even in the animal world there are many murderers and robbers, like the Magpie, these are all natural. The objective is to live in harmony with Nature and not to delude ourselves with false image or excuse. Imbalances made by Humans should be corrected. Those that make 'religions' from the Tao, Christ, Buddha, or any other reflection of The Way may be weak and some even foolish, they hide behind images, not able or afraid to look deeper into life and its relationships, maybe not wanting to take the time or the first step. Those that fear to explore, those that fear other people's beliefs whether because of their own ignorance or something they have been told by some "leader", these people are lost. The only thing to fear is fear itself. The way to do is to be and even all of these words are superfluous if

79

they have not served their purpose, to enlighten. This is what the philosophy of Tao does, enlightens.

Get Words Right.

Please do not call Taoism a religion. Religion could be said to be one of the oldest forms of predatory Human action known, if it is used wrongly. The predator relies upon the fear and ignorance of the victim in order to intimidate with threats of "hell, fire and brimstone" if they do not "support the faith". This, as any enlightened person knows, is totally ridiculous. Each individual has the power to be good or bad or indifferent to degrees. Those that are caught in this web of deceit are usually at a point in their lives where they begin to "feel a need for something greater" than themselves. Youth gives way to age and experience and those that have something worthwhile learn to share and get on with life while others distract themselves with falsehoods, fashions, fiction, food and fads.

The only purpose that the Taoist philosophy could have by being called a religion would be to establish an organised centre, or hall where people could come and learn the Taoist Arts and philosophy in an orderly manner. In some countries, you would have to register it as a religion to get help or tax relief! Help centres would be made more financially workable by being classified as a religious or charitable group. Not totally a bad thing I feel, especially if one could provide a quality venue. Words have little meaning and so classifications not that important to the dedicated scholar, and you do not have to teach it as a religion.

It is the quality of life which counts and right now we need something which will improve the quality of our lives on this tiny planet. All around us we can not only see but hear and feel the destructive tendencies of the human race. Misuse of weapons, money rules, advertising and futile products which cause ill health or insatiably insane people, the greed of politicians who use their positions to make money and not better lives for those who voted them in, drugs that warp the mind or make the user die slowly and painfully from the inside (illegal and legal), petty bureaucracy which creates more paperwork and more jobs and more confusion but still does not get the job done right... oh must I go on, it is so depressing. We need something which improves the quality of life by improving the quality of the individual. There are old sayings from Confucius that sum up some of the flaws in mankind; and when we say "mankind" we also mean "womankind" too.

"He who exercises government by means of his virtue may be compared to the north polar star, which keeps its place and all the other stars turn towards it."

"In a country well governed, poverty is something to be ashamed of. In a country badly governed, wealth is something to be ashamed of."

"The superior man understands what is right; the inferior man understands what will sell."

Confucius or Kong Fuxi portrayed by unknown Artist.

CHAPTER SIX

You & Me - Actions and Reactions
The psychology of "ripples".

When we do or say something, by our actions or words we use are creating another step along an endless, invisible pathway. To use an analogy, it is rather like the game called Dominoes, you can change the direction of the laying-path during play. So can the next player. There may be many instances when we might like to understand the Tao of *our* actions.

Some people study the ways of the Human Mind. It seems that many of these people, including the professionals, are doing this toward a better understanding of themselves, which is not always a bad thing. If we all understood what we said and did, how this affected both our own lives and those around us, then the world might be a far better place. As it is, there are far too many actions and words carried out in haste. How well do you understand yourself ?

If you have studied the way of the Mind, then you may have come across this kind of scenario:

At some point you are talking about a news item "The Army troops are being transported home from the new Peace Zone today." As the conversation continues, you suddenly remember something which you must tell Jessica. "Old Fred says, your bicycle will be ready for Saturday morning, Jessica."

Somewhere in your brain, bits of information zapped around from cell-to-cell and you collated all pieces of information that were connected with <u>transport</u>. If you could see it as a train of thoughts (no pun intended!), then it could be happening something like this;

INPUT: Army troops being transported home today...

THROUGHPUT: ... Army-troops-transport-home

Army-transport-tanks-personnel-carrier-transport-people-going somewhere-people-bus-transport-wheels-bicycle-Fred-Jessica... "Aha!"

The information was stored in only a small location in your brain's memory because it was new and fresh. The more you think about a subject the more locations it will be stored in. If you think about nothing else but Football, then you are likely to know a lot about that subject, but you may be fairly dull otherwise to others who do not like it. Take, for example, the act of "Memory Man" that is sometimes seen on stage, this "trick" is done through practice. The more practice, the more locations and connections, the more power is built up. It seems simple, but it requires lots of practice and dedication.

These connections are quite normal in everyone. In infants they are feelings and emotions which are connected with experiences. These experiences build up with time, they will 'recognise', through these connections, certain things that they either like (such as being cuddled or amused, Yang/positive) or dislike (being dropped or hit, Yin/negative). In our adult lives - remember there is no division between child and adult, only experience and age; these past connections go much, much deeper. All of those things which we experienced (seen, heard, read, felt, touched, et cetera), will play an important part in our actions and reactions later in life. This will apply to any form of stimuli, active or passive. How does this work ?

Imagine you are being introduced to someone whom you have never met before. As this person looks at you, speaks, moves, shakes hands with you, you pick-up on little signals. Some of these are body language, others sounds, intonations of speech, emphasis on certain words, et cetera. Some things you may not like. These are probably associated with, so called, "bad experiences" that you had in the past. Perhaps there was a well practised but insincere phrase that reminded you of someone who 'fooled' you deliberately. The experience of being caught out a few times builds up on those stored connections. You automatically took stock of the situation and then sub-consciously made the decision that you did not trust this new person. This is a fairly common scenario. I think it correct to say that there are a equal number of men and women who are accurate with these instinctive assessments. Those poor souls who are not, they are often caught unawares by others who would use them only for personal gains. These people we call Confidence Tricksters, simply because they trick people who place their confidence in them. "Con Men" or "Con Women", generally "Con Artists", the names by which they are known. Some of the Confidence Tricksters do it as a craft, their trade, so to speak, as that is the way they see it. Others do it almost unwittingly; e.g. some girls go out with some "interesting" men just to experiment and do not see the harm in it, after all, they are just absorbing experiences; that's the way that they see it. Some men go out with what they see as "sexy" girls just to exercise their self-believed physical prowess and boost their misplaced confidence. They do not see the harm in it either. What do we do to each other with this lack of thinking, or do to others who may be involved unwittingly? The more often people receive the shock of being 'conned' or used, in one way or another, the more standoffish they can become and the more these experiences are duplicated and stored in active memory locations. The deeper the affect is and the longer it haunts your Mind.

This is the part of Psychology that becomes Psychiatry; trying to understand and fix mental health issues.

Let us not forget those positive experiences as well. What about when someone who loved you gave you a beautiful flower. What a romantic feeling it produced, to know that someone cared and thought of you even while they were away from you. Perhaps another time, another person in your life came along. They make you feel good and you are thinking of this while you are apart, so what do you do to show them your affection, you pick them a fresh, vibrant bloom. There are many other instances, too. Being helped across a busy road with a heavy or awkward load. Finding the patience to teach and encourage a small child, as someone did with you once. All these things and more created a pleasurable experience which is then locked into a memory location and may be recalled in several ways, by differing stimuli. One of the major distinctions between a positive and a negative experience is this:

> •A negative (Yin) experience is often one-sided, in the example of a 'con' or abused relationship, one person feels dejected and imposed upon, the other simply sees it as a normal reaction and resumes the search for a new 'victim' or experience, consciously or not.

> •A positive (Yang) experience is often two-sided. One person does a good deed and feels good for having done it. The second person feels that someone cares and is also uplifted by the experience.

As you can imagine (Imagination is another perception derived from experience - Yang), all those who have been 'conned' or hurt, can shut themselves off (Yin) to degrees, becoming less trusting, loving or helpful. This can have a multiple rebound effect on many with whom they come into contact. If this negative action is allowed to continue unchecked, then a rather 'edgy' atmosphere can become apparent. This is very obvious in most large cities and towns. So think about your actions, think about the Yin and Yang effects that they may have. We are all responsible for everything that we do and, like the ripples on a pond when a small stone is dropped into the water, the ripples expand outwards to the shore, then they rebound and cross with other ripples. Meanwhile the stone has begun another journey.

In connection with philosophy and psychology, I am often reminded of a philosophic conversation between Master Po and his young student, 'Grasshopper' at the Shaolin Temple in China. This was, of course, in the TV. series called 'Kung Fu', starring David Carradine.

Grasshopper (G) sits by a pool, into the middle he tosses a small pebble. Master Po (MP) approaches quietly.

M.P. "Where does your pebble walk to, Grasshopper?"

G. "It walks…(?) …it's journey is to nowhere."

M.P. "Each journey begins and also ends."

G. "Then the ending is the bottom of the pool."

M.P. "Does not the pebble, entering the water, begin fresh journeys?"

G. (Pauses for thought) "It seems unceasing."

M.P. "Such is the journey through life. It begins, it ends, yet fresh journeys go forth. Young Cane, when I was a boy, I fell into a hole in the ground and I was broken and could not climb out. I might have died there, but a stranger came along and saved me. He said it was his obligation, that for help he had once received, he must in return help ten others, each of whom must also then help ten others. So that good deeds would spread out like the ripples from a pebble in a pond. I was one of his ten, and you became one of mine. I pass on this obligation to you."

So it is that the psychology of human life is involved with philosophy. The thoughts of Confucius are carried forward into Taoism, many of the ideals and thoughts of Taoism were ported into Buddhism. Each has their own style, but they all share the same things, which is Moral Values.

A society without moral values is often called "decadent". The name though is not really important, just a label for scholars to play with. What is important is what Confucius brought to the table, and that was "family values". This idea was so popular with the Chinese people that it even permeated the Art of Chinese Boxing (slang. "Kung-fu"). That went like this:

Titles of rank -
Grandmaster = Shih-Jo (Teacher-Great Grandfather)
Master = Shih-Jo (Teacher Grandfather)
Teacher = Shih-fu (Teacher-Father)

Then students, regardless of actual age, would be ranked as the children, who all had younger or older brothers and sisters, depending on when they joined the group.

This emphasis on family values has been neutralised now, under modernised systems, and replaced with rather bland titles that could be used for any tradesman. The old way gave family values first priority, so building up the strength in believing that family respectfulness is of high importance, not following a political agenda like blind sheep.

The key to change is through education, *in all things*. Not "brainwashing", but proper education which starts with the family, with Mother and Father, then Uncles and Aunts, Grandparents too. Traditionally many children would be left with Grandparents while Mum and Dad went out to work. The wisdom of the older generations would often be imparted to the children, as would manners, respect and the importance of being helpful. What we seem to have now are world-wide societies that have been separated from this pattern by many means, over many decades. The implementing of laws, false social standards whereby parents are told their children must go to a state run school, just at the age when they are most able to absorb knowledge, but then learn what the State wants to teach them, which usually omits family respect and such good society values, but includes doing as they are told and not asking questions, be a champion for the state, not for family, etc. This kind of education creates segregation and, to some extent, selfishness.

When we speak of the philosophy and the effect that it has on the person or persons who learn it, we are talking about "harmony". Tao is in harmony; despite what some people see as negative issues, such as Tsunami, Comet damage, exploding nebula and volcanoes. These are all very natural, the problem is that humans have bred too much and in desperation to find a place to live, build houses far too close to the shoreline, or far too close to volcanoes. This is not the fault of Tao or Nature, it is the unthinking fault of some Human Nature; not all, just some. There is even an old Chinese proverb for this phenomena, which can be applied to studying or training, or many other factors:

"Never build your house on sand"!

There has probably been enough said on the "actions and reactions" aspect. The problems are global, as we see on News channels most of the time... but, hold on. While we are thinking "globally" we are missing what is right under our very nose, the *parochial* aspect and, even more importantly *family*. This is how we change the world; remember Confucius's verse from earlier?

If there is righteousness in the heart,

there will be righteousness in the home.

Righteousness in the home will spawn.

Righteousness in the community;

if there is righteousness in the community

there will be righteousness in the towns.

If there is righteousness in the towns

there will be righteousness in the world.

(Confucius)

This is one of the keystones of morality and social order (as opposed to social chaos) in Taoism. The philosophy of Tao is not just about Nature, as in Space, flowers and other things we see around us, but about Human Nature.

Make no mistake, Humans are not the brightest species on this planet! If they were, then all the madness we see around us would not exist. You, him, her and quite a few others, are not a part of that madness. You are reading this book because you care about what is happening and feel that there must be something else to life than just following the sheep to the feeding station. There is.

CHAPTER SEVEN

The TAO of Martial Arts

Most people probably think of Martial Arts as just a way of learning how to defend yourself if attacked. In the West, in particular, many schools of Martial Arts have opened up since the TV series 'Kung Fu' hit the screens in the late 60's (USA) and early 70's (UK). Most though are just fight schools. Not many have a philosophy behind them, such as genuine traditional T'ai chi Ch'uan or Taoist Ch'uan-shu (Taoist Kung-fu) schools do.

THE TAO OF CH'UAN-SHU (TAOIST KUNG-FU).

T'ien Ti Tao (The Way of Heaven & Earth™) Kung-fu is often referred to as being an 'internal' school of Chinese Boxing but this reference is not always understood, nor is it entirely accurate. T'ai Chi Ch'uan is supposed to represent the two opposite forces of Yin and Yang (Tao) to create a balanced exercise and therefore a 'balanced' practitioner. Not all T'ai Chi Ch'uan schools, or teachers, relay the whole thing. It appears that this corruption may occur for many reasons, best explained by them, but sometimes due to neglect of the governing principles (Tao) being present, sometimes one is over emphasised, sometimes a student leaves his Master before he has the whole system (impatience or lack of wits?). T'ien Ti Tao training is, fundamentally, true "T'ai Chi Ch'uan" or "Supreme Polarity Boxing" - that is what the school's name means. TTT is fully aware of most modern people's needs in training. From the outset the practitioner who is generally unfit has their health built up to a much better level, so we start off with Yang training. The person who already does some form of physical training benefits too, they are made more supple and excessive aggression may be channeled off into beneficial forms. So right from the start the correct balance is applied and the trainee should feel positive gains almost immediately.

The TTT training follows a syllabus which takes the student through Yang training at the beginning to Yin training at the other end. Each part though has its own Yin and Yang elements. This is proper balance and the practitioner should be able to flux and flow freely between Yin and Yang. In fact the whole body exhibits subtle, or obvious, Yin and Yang movements. A mature student develops and uses more Ch'i and may be more concerned with healing and philosophy than fighting. At the higher levels Jin is produced.

The early Easterner, through lack of technical toys or gadgets to distract him, was much more deeply involved in the pursuit of knowledge, social reform and spiritual growth. So Martial Arts were not a "be all and end all" but often used as a tool to keep fit and gain better mental and physical health whilst enjoying the offshoot abilities to defend one's self or perform better physical tasks. The philosophy and relationships to other activities in life were also pursued and studied by most. This was almost confined to the Orient and China in particular. However, the only thing which is constant is change. All things do and must change, just like night and day, the seasons of the years, growth, death and decay. Whereas we in the Western Hemisphere are now feeling the effect of a burned-out Industrial Revolution that really took-off in the days when Queen Victoria ruled the soot, in the East (Orient) they are now being effected by the shock-wave of the Technical Industrial explosion. It is now their turn to exploit our findings and to improve their own creature comforts. So once more Nature's Way has placed the metaphoric Yin/Yang boot is on the other foot. This now leaves us (in the West) with much more time to sit and contemplate the answers to life, the Universe and everything.

To help us in our quest for knowledge of such a deep and mysterious nature we need some guidelines or pointers. Better still, a simple science that instead of making things harder to understand makes them easier by using, say, simple analyses and comparison with basic, everyday elements. Taoism does this. As we can see from the simplified descriptions contained within this succinct yet expansive book.

The philosophy of Yin and Yang is most often associated with Taoist practices. Buddhism (Mahayana - the wider vehicle of study) and Taoism are closely linked in many aspects, (Zen or Ch'an being one religion where the two elements can be seen to merge) as you could discover from many other reference sources. The philosophy of Yin and Yang is used to teach the basic ideas of Nature's dual polarity (negative and positive influences) to students of The Way. Other descriptive factors also come into play; The Five Elements (Wu Hsing).

There are many unseen forces at work which we can describe as either Yin or Yang actions which are either pure forces (e.g.; negative or positive) or elemental. Most are likely to be a mixture of both. Heaven is Yang and Earth is Yin. Heaven appears to be empty, yet it supports the Earth and other planets which are solid and heavy. The Sun is hot and dense liquid but it also is supported by that which is cold and weightless. How can this be? Space, as we call it, is not exactly empty. There are forces at work which we can not see with our physical eyes, but they are there just the same. There are centrifugal and centripetal forces acting on the stars and planets, magnetic, electrical and other forces which beam and pulse their ways into the scheme of things. All of these being invisible to the human eye. But if one is 'sensitive' some of these forces may be felt as a strong presence. Some may even be aware of the effect of these forces, or similar, on and within the human body. I recall that in recent years a couple of astronomers tried to figure out why light from a distant star was being seen even though a small planet blocked it's path. They found that energy fields were "bending" the light around the planet's surface. These energy fields had previously been unseen. These are also Qi.

Apart from the Earth's gravity, the main forces we are concerned with in any exercise or boxing practice are Li (hard energy, kinetic) and ch'i (soft energy, intrinsic) which are both developed and used differently. In brief the differences may be summed up thus:

- Kinetics - the science of the action of force in producing or changing motion - Li energy.

- Intrinsic - belonging to the internal; essential; belonging to the point at issue - Qi energy.

(N.B. Here I have used the definitions within the dictionary as a proper translation from the original Chinese would be too ambiguous).

Understanding kinetic energy is quite straight forward, but Ch'i.... a different story altogether, and one that has caused many disagreements. Ch'i is actually a mixture of energies: infrared microwaves, electromagnetic energy and static electricity being the main ingredients. The existence of this force complete with its negative and positive polarities has been proven by medical scientists. In tests using ultra-sensitive electronic sensors they measured the flow of ch'i in all of the body's 'Meridians' (the invisible channels that carry ch'i around the body and are present on everyone) and were also able to verify the existence of 'the points' as used in acupuncture: these seem to convert, boost and/or redirect the ch'i.

The practice of ch'i kung ("Qi-gong", energy training) is rightly only associated with certain internal Kung-fu systems (although crude forms may exist in some external styles). These are known as 'The Internal Arts' or the "Sister Arts" because of their Yin training features. They fall loosely into three categories: (1) Hsing-I Ch'uan, (2) Pa Kua Ch'uan, and (3) T'ai Chi Ch'uan. Each has its own particular style of movement and all three Arts are often taught under the same roof. What is more, each one of the three styles concentrates on a different aspect of the Tao, Yin/Yang, Five Elements, flux and flow, et cetera. (T'ien Ti Tao Kuoshu is compatible with all of these principles and also features many of the exercises which are in the essence of the others). Each of these exercises has its own peculiar effect upon the practitioner, physical, physiological and even psychological.

The two categories of Chinese Boxing which are loosely placed under the descriptions of Yin and Yang are known as 'Hard Style' (Yang) and 'Soft Style' (Yin). A rough description follows.

EXTERNAL (HARD) KUNG-FU.

External or hard style was well suited to Military usage and the exponents are expected within about three years to have reached their peak in trained ability. It emphasises the development of the chest and arms, development of muscle and using the force of the limbs to strike with. It does not use ch'i to any worthwhile degree, although some teachers incorporate certain breathing exercises (usually with dynamic tension) and call it an 'internal' or ch'i kung form. This is not entirely inaccurate as ch'i kung loosely means Energy Training using breathing practices and of these there are many Forms or exercises.

Hard style, like all forms of athletic endeavour, is practically impossible to keep up as one gets much older as it concentrates upon muscles and by the very nature of "external" exercise (by neglecting the internal organs and functions which build and heal tissue) it tends to destroy that which it has built. The joints may be the first to go as many of the "hard" styles encourage the locking out of the elbows or knees when punching or kicking. Some can also be very linear in style and do not concentrate on economics of technique - power is sometimes wasted for the sake of style or power maybe comes only from the limbs individually, not the whole body. Many movements are longer reaching (as in Wu Shu), probably because they were developed for use against staff, spear or other weapons and were styled on "big styles" like Northern Chang Ch'uan.

INTERNAL (SOFT) KUNG-FU.

Just as much of a challenge through the endurance, both physical and mental, needed to get it right, the internal styles are based on self-defence within the environment concerned. This may differ slightly in legal requirements or terrain (e.g.; city, village, rocky ground, living on a boat...) as well as the founder's background in Kung-fu. It usually emphasises all-round development, balance, self-control, the use of skill, circular motion and mind/body harmony. Strikes are backed-up by the whole of the body and often seem more powerful than 'muscle pushed' strikes.

The 'soft fist' stylist will often turn the attacker's power to his or her own advantage at an unexpected moment. With the skilled internal stylist the ch'i (intrinsic energy) can be used in many ways to upset the attacker' equilibrium. But not just anyone will be taught these methods, of course. A wise precaution!

NOTE: Though the word 'Internal' is frequently used it does not necessarily follow that it is correct. Usually it is used as a generalisation. Nei Kung is "internal training" and is most accurately applied to those practises such as Ch'i Kung (Qi-gong) and other therapeutic exercises designed to prevent ill-health and cure disease. Most Martial Arts or self-defence systems contain both Nei Kung and Wei Kung as muscle and ch'i combine in work.

Yin exercises can be used to create Yang effects on the body-system and vice-versa. Thus the science of Tao may be used to create the desired effect in one's training. Confusion is often caused by this aspect though, as it hard for the average person to understand how it all works. This book is not the place.

Equilibrium (T'ien Ti Tao's motto in all of its senses) may be gained not only from the varied exercise routines but also from the learning of the techniques used in self-defence. Some of these are linear but as a rule of thumb they are circular. Spirals, crescents and arcs of all sizes. Still retaining the previous descriptions of the properties of Yin and Yang we can now add some more. These relate directly to boxing technique.

Yang: hard, direct, forceful and persistent.

Yin: soft, indirect, gentle and persuasive.

When we first begin training or are very young we tend to use too much physical force and muscle (Yang). This becomes most apparent with the majority of teenagers who train, as they are more aware of the physical aspects of their own growing bodies. This is a shame because as you get older you may have already set in "the rot, so to speak, and laid the foundations for injury and disability later on in life; the age when you become aware that these Internal systems have much more to offer. This is the blindness of the teenage years. As we get older or the muscle-power declines we tend to use more skill (Yin) to empower the physical ability (Yang). In T'ien Ti Tao Ch'uan-shu skill is emphasised from the start and using 'total body power', as opposed to the power of one limb or muscle group only. Even a basic linear strike can be made more effective if the rest of the body can be employed to make it appear to turn a corner. The withdrawal of the punching or kicking limb can also be made to alter its owner's direction as well as being able to act as a block or deflection. Using these methods the hindrance of ch'i can also be avoided. This is an ideal Art for younger people, those in their early teens, as can teach good sense, ability, skill, economy of movement whilst achieving far greater power and much more besides.

To give you some idea of how the Yin/Yang forces interplay in Kung-fu I have devised the following diagram:

(A - left) Mr. Yang in the white T-shirt attacks Mr. Yin with a straight right punch to the chest.

(B - right) Mr. Yin side-steps to his own left in Left Extension Stance to avoid the punch. At the same time he uses a left Palm Block to deflect Mr. Yang's punch and upset his balance.

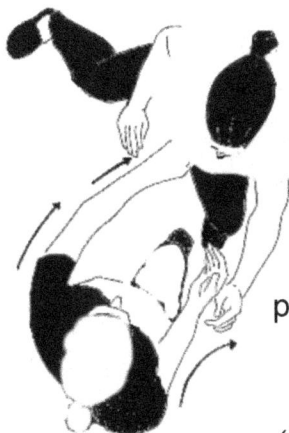

(C, left) Mr. Yang, being persistent, retracts his right hand and uses it to sweep Mr. Yin's left arm away to the side.

Simultaneously Mr. Yang turns his waist clockwise and

punches with his left fist to knock Mr. Yin off-balance.

(NOTE: Although not illustrated here, Mr. Yin could regain the advantage by using his right hand to Palm block the punch and then 'bridge' Mr. Yang's arms. This would leave Mr. Yin in the position to counter-attack.) There are many more limitless combinations possible.

The Heaven and Earth (Yang and Yin) Forms and auxiliary techniques teach subtle, sound and economic defence/counter strategies. Hard forces are met with soft and weaknesses with strengths. The opponents will find themselves launching attacks that never get to their target and will then suddenly be overwhelmed and thrown off balance by the use of subtle skills.

To be too hard or too soft is also an imbalance that should be avoided in training. The practitioner, through constant and dedicated training, knows instinctively when to generate power, how much, what kind or when to conceal it. He will also be able to absorb power, transmute it and recycle it at will.

In a world where business men/women try to sell you bigger muscles how can you develop a body which looks rounded, softly curved (not heavily muscularly defined), very strong and is as tough as old boots, just by doing breathing, stretching, general physical and meditation exercises? How come that the slower, more contemplative and precise self-defence exercises can lead to lightning fast reactions? We harness complete body power, not just muscles.

A lot here though depends upon proper teaching methods, too. It may be all to easy for a teacher to loose inspiration, forget what he/she has been taught or simply omit some of the more subtle elements of training - as do many students when practising. Many people are distracted by Martial Arts sales talk and are foolishly led to believe that another style has a magic technique that will turn them into a super-person. What we emphasise in T'ien Ti Tao is the knowledge that is behind the techniques and exercises. A craftsman must be fully familiar with all aspects of his subject, tools and materials before being able to make a masterpiece.

To end this chapter without mentioning the effects of 'imbalanced' training, I feel, would be a travesty of Tao. The person that discards the balanced approach for another is likely to suffer the consequences in the end. Take as an example one who is attracted to a particular style of Kung-fu because of its use of violent techniques and development of muscles. This is Yang toward the extremes. Such training prolonged would eventually burn out the practitioner or maybe even induce them to a more aggressive lifestyle. The after effects of this can come out in many negative ways, from violence and family abuse, drugs or alcohol, through to other less obvious psychological traits such as constant criticism of friends, family or just anything.

Training in less physical methods could lead to becoming weak bodied, recluse, lacking in any sort of confidence and withdrawn generally. This person may allow himself to become the target of the former type of person, either physically or mentally. If left unchecked for too long the effects of extreme Yin can cause a sudden outburst (Yang) in which years of hidden frustrations erupt like a dormant volcano. So a Yang person can become hostile, over-ambitious, outspoken, tense and stressed. While the Yin person may show signs of being withdrawn, isolated, vulnerable to extremes, very nervous, unadventurous and inactive. If a good balance is maintained in all things then there should be no major imbalances and a wide spectrum of pure and natural emotions should be openly displayed. When Yin and Yang work in harmony peace prevails and there is no cause for concern.

There is no room for ego, either. The balanced man or woman has no room for false pride, bullying others or extorting favours by pretence. That which is not given freely is regretted and 'karma' knows its own debts. Karma is the unwritten law which is depicted by the old saying, "live by the sword, die by the sword!". So what good is a well balanced exercise/lifestyle to you? Well, if harmony is not what you want then it is no good to you. If however you wish for a better balanced life with less stress, more understanding and sincere friends then the answer is "everything".

Competition, had to be mentioned, as when a person competes they want to prove themselves against others, to "be the best", etcetera. The true Martial Artist does not compete; s/he may spar, grapple or fight to get the better outcome against an attacker, but not compete.

The reality is that the only person that has to be beaten is yourself, your own insecurities or ego. When you compete you compete with yourself. Address all things without bent or prejudice. We have had a couple of students who entered National Competition, for different reasons, one woman came 2nd in the entire UK Nationals; Michelle "Bouncing Bomb" Rooke.

The Teacher - Student Relationship

A good teacher should have been a good student and had to start from the beginning, taking time to study hard and well. A good student is one who practices all that he is shown and more, discovering the Tao of each step. This should be remembered.

A student should be respectful of anyone who has studied a subject longer than themselves, especially the teacher and the teacher's teacher (the Master) and the Master's teacher, et cetera.

Student's should be patient and determined, they should listen and observe quietly and not look for "quick progress", for this is the sign of a poor student who is impatient and impetuous. Do not expect your teacher to do all the work and study for you. He will make you work hard: an old saying is that a student is like a piece of good quality metal, the teacher a blacksmith who beats, shapes and makes useful tool out of it!

A student who did not work hard enough outside of classes once asked, "Shih-fu. I am am not progressing with this technique. Can you help me with something which would make it easier?" The teacher replied, "I am only the signpost that points to The Way, you must walk the path yourself".

Most people think that Martial Arts is all about fighting. It may look that way, and at the same time, it depends heavily on the school. Kickboxing is not "Martial Arts", exactly; various techniques taken from MA and Boxing, Wrestling, etcetera. Martial Arts is any school of self-defence which has a Syllabus, and that syllabus is designed to instruct from Beginner to Instructor and beyond. The syllabus will contain suitable and appropriate exercises which will increase fitness, strength, flexibility, determination and self-control, plus at the same time time preparing the student for what he or she will be learning in regards of technique and sparring.

Learning any technique requires the student to watch, listen and then copy the Instructor; who she/he sees as their worthy senior, so acts respectfully towards. This respect then builds up into trust and confidence; the Teacher will be keeping a watchful eye on students and should address any issues of ego, disrespect or negative behaviour of any sort.

After about ten years, the student should be close to making a teaching grade. But there is always "polishing up" to be done, new techniques and methods to learn; as well as possible meditations, health practices, healing techniques and more, so never assume you now know everything!

The act of learning any technique requires this same process - look, listen, understand, then copy - then practice, practice, practice, practice!

"A journey of Ten Thousand Miles begins with just one step."

It is this process, above, which makes the student *think*. Thinking like this is like Computer programming, it is done in logical steps, not missing out any detail. The student's brain then becomes conditioned, ordered, more logical. This also means it is less random, disordered or illogical. This is psychology possibly at its finest level, where one person can do something which makes them think and act in a logical and ordered manner, seeing situations as they are, step-by-step and resolving issues in their life.

Not only are the psychological effects of Martial Arts training the normally unseen benefits, but the social aspects are too. It has long been known in the world of Traditional Martial Arts that highly trained Martial Artists become useful members of the community.

Taoist Kung-fu (including Trad. T'ai Chi Ch'uan/Taijiquan) is slightly different again, as the student will learn about balance, harmony and gradually get to understand the relationships of various elements, including human interaction, of course. It has similar mental effects.

The current era, year 2000 onwards, has been a worrying era for many older people who have seen many changes, but also understand what consequences specific changes can bring. Many Traditional Arts instructors have expressed concern over younger generations' lack of appreciation or respect for anything traditional. They do not understand that "traditional", in the sense of martial Arts, philosophy, etcetera, is not being "part of the system", but understanding society and having your own logically trained mind to be able to recognise what is happening around you, and make sense of it. Traditional, when in respect of training, means "well thought through" or "established by reason of positive effect", it has nothing to do with the perceived "System", government or even age; bar the amount of years that the syllabus has taken to be perfected, of course. An old saying in the traditional Arts is, "Easily gained, quickly lost." Meaning that the longer time spent studying something the longer you will keep it.

The world-wide scene of Martial Arts has been torn apart almost by egotistic young men and women who think that they know best, despite their frugal years of life and lack of experience. This has brought about a spate of misnomer "Martial Arts", MMA and Exercise classes, often given trendy new names like "Fusion", or "Extreme", styles mainly inspired by going through two or three books, or a handful of classes, and trying to "mix and match" exercises or techniques, often taught poorly; again, through lack of experience.

In reality, there is *nothing* that has not already been done before. Many of these new breed, DIY group leaders have no qualifications; and by that I mean they have not actually gone from Beginner to Teacher/2nd Degree Black Belt, in any other system, so they do not have an idea about progressive steps; often they realise that they have to "learn on the fly" (learn on the job), otherwise more experienced people in their classes may show them up to be not what they say they are.

Having those logical steps, the well thought through syllabus, can never be replaced. Random training produces random minds. Random minds cannot order their own life. Chaos follows.

Imagine.
If *proper*, traditional Martial Arts was taught at all schools, it would help resolve many of the issues of modern society. It requires mindfulness, ordered thinking which in turn creates self-control.

We would see far less bullying, less mental health issues, less general health issues and less antisocial behaviour in the streets or homes.

CHAPTER EIGHT

THE TAO of CHINESE HOROSCOPES

Most of us are familiar with the Western Zodiac and the signs used to describe them. There are Capricorn - The Goat, Aquarius - The Water Bearer, Pisces - The Fishes, Aries - The Ram, Taurus - The Bull, Gemini - The Twins, Cancer - The Crab, Leo - The Lion, Virgo - The Virgin, Libra - The Scales, Scorpio - The Scorpion and Sagittarius - The Beast/Bow-Man. These signs are related to their supposed or imagined star formation shapes, which can be seen in the night sky. Each has a ruling planet, a gemstone, colours and numbers which all relate to the person born under that sign. There may be other signs influences upon the individual, according to the position of the other planets, in relation to the first, at the time of birth. These influences are called rising signs or ascendants.

The Chinese lunar calendar has the longest chronological record in history. It dates from 2,637 years B.C. (our Gregorian Calendar) when the reigning Emperor, Huang-Di, introduced it; as you will recall from earlier parts of the book, he was also responsible for many other important introductions. The first cycle began in his 61st year of reign. Each cycle lasts 60 years and during this cycle each of the twelve animal signs (often referred to as Earth Branches) is combined with one of the Five Elements (Wu Hsing). These are: Wood - ruled by Jupiter, Fire - ruled by Mars, Earth - ruled by Saturn, Metal - ruled by Venus and Water - ruled by Mercury.

The Five Elements are further divided by the principle of Yin and Yang, thus having Negative and Positive years within the cycle, e.g.; + Fire year followed by a - Fire year.

There are many similarities between the two systems, I would call them "crossovers", for they seem to intertwine mysteriously, like the great symbol of Yin and Yang itself. When doing a reading I would often point out that there may be an inclination of the person's character toward one system's translation or the other. But on the whole I prefer to study the Five Elements of the person's Chinese

Zodiac, finding this usually more accurate in portraying possible traits. More about this later.

Folk-lore has it that as Lord Buddha (Siddhartha Gautama) lay dying, 12 animals came to pay their respects. As a reward for their loyalty and friendship he named a year after each one. These were to be repeated in a constant cycle. First came the Rat, then the Ox, Tiger, Rabbit, Dragon, Snake, Horse, Sheep, Monkey, Rooster, Dog and Boar. Whichever year you were born in has one of these animals as its 'ruler', this (according to the Chinese Zodiac) will be, "The animal which hides in your heart." The Chinese ascendant signs are dictated by the hour in which you were born, another one of the animal influences combined with an element. There are a total of Five Influences in your chart, as follows:

YEAR = ANIMAL + ELEMENT
(Animal of Year and Year Element)

FIXED = ANIMAL + ELEMENT
(Each animal has a Fixed Element)

HOUR = ANIMAL + ELEMENT
(One of the 12 animals - in 2 hr Segments)

MONTH = ANIMAL + ELEMENT
(Month animal related to Western Zodiac)

COUNTRY = ANIMAL + ELEMENT
(Dictated by the year the Ruler was enthroned in your country)

All the years are preset and follow on in endless cycles. To give you an idea, some are reproduced below. You will notice that the year does not begin on January 1st, as does the Gregorian year. The dates will vary slightly from year-to-year, but generally fall in January or February.

RAT February 10, 1948 to January 28, 1949 - Earth (+)

OX January 29, 1949 to February 16, 1950 - Earth (-)

TIGER February 17, 1950 to February 5, 1951 - Metal (+)

RABBIT February 6, 1951 to January 26, 1952 - Metal (-)

DRAGON January 27, 1952 to February 13, 1953 - Water (+)

SNAKE February 14, 1953 to February 2, 1954 - Water (-)

HORSE February 3, 1954 to January 23, 1955 - Wood (+)

SHEEP January 24, 1955 to February 11, 1956 - Wood (-)

MONKEY February 12, 1956 to January 30, 1957 - Fire (+)

ROOSTER January 31, 1957 to February 17, 1958 - Fire (-)

DOG February 18, 1958 to February 7, 1959 - Earth (+)

BOAR February 8, 1959 to January 27, 1960 - Earth (-)

(This represents One-Fifth of a complete cycle.)

As stated earlier, the year that you were born in is governed by "the animal that hides in your heart", but that is not what we are concerned with here. We are taking a closer look at the TAO of Chinese Horoscopes, the YIN and YANG of the Five Elements and how this can effect your life.

Each of the five elements has a negative and positive reflection. We call this a Creative Cycle and Controlling Cycle. It is easy to see how each of the elements can either stimulate or pacify the next. Look at the chart below, this is the same Chart or Diagram used in TCM or the general philosophy, by which we can see which event or "Element" is causing another event, or "symptom".

ELEMENTARY CYCLE OF STIMULATION (CREATION)

FIRE creates EARTH creates METAL creates WATER creates WOOD creates FIRE.

ELEMENTARY CYCLE OF PACIFICATION (CONTROL)

FIRE controls METAL controls WOOD controls EARTH controls WATER controls FIRE.

In your own personal life these elements can work for you or against you. There are so many combinations of elements that may be found within your own personal chart, that it can be quite complex or fairly simple. But if you take the main element, that is the element of your birth year, followed by the element which is fixed and then the hour of birth element, then this will give you the best indication. Do not forget or discard the elements that are to found in your Western Chart, though. This can sometimes explain a "pull" or behavioural trait that might seem otherwise "slightly out of alignment" with your Chinese Chart. I always surmise that the two to go hand-in-hand together. Theodora Lau and Laura Lau in the excellent 'Handbook of Chinese Horoscopes' (ISBN 9780285644312) presents the east-west mix admirably and, in my opinion, is very accurate at describing the characters born under those signs.

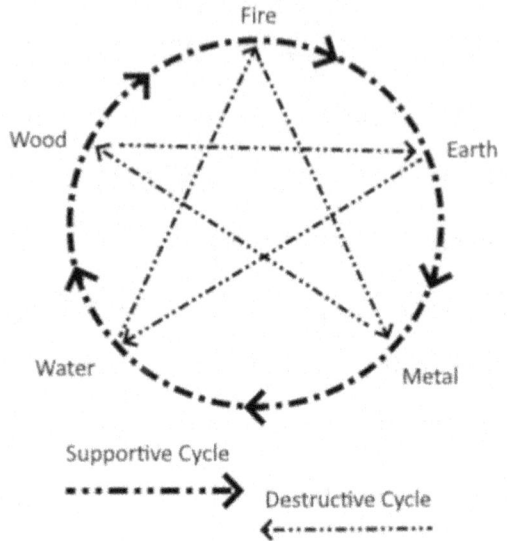

The Five Elements / Wu Hsing

Fire
Wood
Earth
Water
Metal

Supportive Cycle
Destructive Cycle

So how do the elements affect your life, career or relationships? First you need to know your own elements, then those of your wife/husband, lover, children, boss or what-have-you. The next chart shows you a simple left-to-right compatibility table. Find your element at the left and look across the table to see whom you will conflict with and whom you will be in harmony with. You will also see those elements which are neutral, offering "NO CONFLICT". Refer to the CREATIVE & CONTROLLING cycles and you will understand the "SUCCESS" elements easier. Take, for example, the element of FIRE, it has no conflict with other FIRE elements, but because FIRE controls METAL and is generated by WOOD this gives successful relationships. But, if you partner in life is METAL, be warned, they may not like to be controlled by you! Likewise, watch out for those born under the WATER sign, they may dampen your FIRE just a little too much!

YOUR ELEMENT/COMPATIBILITY CHART

YOUR ELEMENT	MAIN CONFLICT	SOME CONFLICT	NO CONFLICT	SUCCESS
METAL	FIRE	EARTH	METAL	WATER/WOOD
FIRE	WATER	EARTH	FIRE	WOOD/METAL
WATER	EARTH	METAL	WATER	FIRE/WOOD
EARTH	WOOD	FIRE	EARTH	WATER/METAL
WOOD	METAL	FIRE	WOOD	EARTH/WATER

This description of the elemental influences upon our lives is also further used to describe the types of career that we may find better or more satisfactory results in. This has been studied, of course, by many in the past but can also be found by us in the present.

EXAMPLES OF TRADE by element:

WOOD: Lumbar, Paper, Furniture, Printing/Publishing, Foodstuffs, etc.

FIRE: Fuels, Energy & Heat, Politics, Creative Leadership, Athletics, etc.

EARTH: Property, Farming, Building, Management, Administration, Detection.

METAL: Canning, Jewellery, Transport Industry, Money, Machines, Tools.

WATER: Public Relations, Teaching, Psychology, Liquid Industry, Shipping.

These are only brief descriptions and serve as a rough guide. Having said that, you may know your element and suddenly see why you have been so unsuccessful at tackling a certain career (or person!) for all these years. Time for a change. Generally the "majority" element in your chart will have the influence, not forgetting the "polarity" (negative or positive) as well. This can make the difference as to how you should approach things. Let us look at a "dummy" chart. (I shall probably get a complaint now from someone actually called Jane Doe on Facebook who says I'm calling her a dummy!)

Jane Doe - Born June 15th 1950 in UK

METAL + = Year of Birth, 1950 (TIGER)

WOOD + = Fixed Animal Element.

FIRE + = Hour of Birth, 11 a.m. to 1 p.m. - Hours of The Horse.

FIRE + = Month Element, June 15th (Gemini/Horse).

WATER + = Country of Birth (UK 1953 Coronation: WATER + /DRAGON).

Jane Doe has a very strong affinity to the triad of TIGER, HORSE and DOG. But apart from that she has Five Yang Stems, making her a very "stubborn, headstrong and argumentative" person indeed! In the first place is METAL +, this controls WOOD + in the second. Wood is the artistic and "growth and expansion" principle. There are two FIRE + in third and fourth places, these may, hopefully, control the hard METAL edge and "forge" a better lifestyle with experience. All-in-all, this person is all "teeth and claws", quick, talkative, maybe too outspoken. Always on the move, vivacious, liable to "attack" for no good reason due to an over-aggressive nature. But she will still appear glamorous, very radical in her beliefs, unorthodox and "not to be tamed" (who'd want to take on this Tiger!).

TEMPERAMENT

The Five Stems (elements) that were mentioned above, are perhaps one of the most important factors determining your personality - I can just hear those with more positive than negative exclaiming, in bold and pithy terms, "Huh! Rubbish! Who does this bloke think he's

kidding? I'm not taking that stuff, I am **not** aggressive... am I?!!!" -
but, all jokes aside, they do relate to your overall personality and
temperament, sometimes very clearly so. Remember that earlier on
in the book we saw how the TAO was split into YIN and YANG, the
Female and Male principles? Bear these in mind, the Yin being
"passive" whilst the Yang is "aggressive". Also keep in mind that
passive does not mean totally yielding and aggressive does not
mean totally arrogant, forceful or belligerent.

The Balance Of Stems:

WOMEN

You require THREE YIN and TWO YANG to have a "balanced"
nature that "portrays the average female temperament". Any more
YIN stems would lead toward a quieter, even timid or retiring nature.
Five could mean that you just sink back into your shell and become
almost hermit-like, all the rush and activity, decisions and flurry of the
world being "just too much".

More than two Yang stems and you may be very active, progressive
and even a busy organiser, hustling people into little groups and
activities. Four and you could be finding it difficult to stay out of
arguments. Five, well, take care and think twice before jumping in
head-long and accusing everyone else of being wrong!

MEN

You require THREE YANG and TWO YIN to have a "balanced"
nature that "portrays the average male temperament". More than this
would lead to a slightly more aggressive personality. Five Yang
stems could be real trouble! Those with five Yang often expect far too
much from others and rarely see that is they who are too demanding.

If you have only two Yang stems then a quieter, even somewhat timid
nature shows, arguments (?), not for you. Five Yin stems could place
you at the mercy of any aggressive male or female that wanted to
take advantage of your withdrawn and hermit-like character. Beware.
Just enjoy the quieter things in life and sit down with a good book.

The Politicians Exposed!
The examples below were done by me when I was asked to lecture at a meeting for some western Astrologers some years ago. The main political characters at the time seemed a good example to use as they were more or less seen in the public eye, on television or in news papers, and were therefore fairly well known for their individual traits. Firstly I explained all the personalities, but without a name attached. As soon as I dropped a clue as the fame of these characters the audience guessed who each was by their traits.

THE CHARACTER

Commentary & Character*:

DAVID STEELE - BORN, Year of Tiger, Hour of Rat. Vivacious, fearless, shrewd and likely to dive in headlong. Too many Yang stems! The elements are well placed for Management, growth and expansion with the controlling Fire in the centre.

NEIL KINNOCK - Born, Year of Tiger, Hour of Sheep. Fiery and defiant, fearless and home-loving. Too many Yang stems! Lots of Fire, but if it were kept below the water, then the resulting energy (like steam) could be put to good use.

MARGARET THATCHER - Born, Year of Ox, Hour of Dragon. Likes to wear the trousers and will not hear of anyone else's opinions. Home organiser. Slightly too Yang. This 'Iron Lady' is really made of wood! I wonder if it was her or Business Investment husband Dennis that made the political policies? There is Artistic growth and expansion here, a certain sternness, but there is a 'lucky' Dragon in the background!

Dr. OWEN - Born, Year of Tiger, Hour of Sheep. (also Cancer/Sheep month). This man is too well balanced to be a politician! He is gentle, protective, non-aggressive and will allow all their rightful say. There is the Wood, constantly "cleaving" the Earth whilst the Negative energy of Fire calmly controls the growth of the Wood. This makes movement rather slow, but calculated.

(This section was written many years back but is still relevant for intents and purposes.)

There you have it, albeit in brief. The YIN and YANG of Chinese Horoscopes. The Chinese believe that if your chart displays tendencies toward, say, Fire, for example, all is not hopeless. To control all that consuming energy (which may cause stress and anxiety) you should surround yourself with the elements that are not in your chart.

So, if *your* chart reads;

FIRE +, FIRE +, METAL - , FIRE - , WATER + , then you could surround yourself with WATER (trips on the river, calming fish-tanks, etcetera) and WOOD (plants, flowers and things that are pleasing to the eye). This should provide some balance and help reduce stress.

WATER signs sometimes may be a little "wishy-washy" and here a FIRE friend might be allowed to "bring them to the boil" occasionally, stimulate the steam! Again, surrounding one's self with WOOD and EARTH (Clay, Bricks - home-, Painting, etcetera) combined with the energies that FIRE has to offer, can be fruitful and balancing.

EARTH souls control water, so they want to get some METAL working for them (Money, Jewels, Cars, etcetera). Water pursuits may provide a welcome break or relaxation.

There is far more to the Chinese Zodiac than can be discussed here. This brief look at the values will give you some glimpse into "the other half" of the Horoscope methods. The TAO of the Chinese Zodiac with its Five Elements and their YIN/YANG values is not something that can be studied or learned overnight. To evaluate this system and its hidden truths, one must carefully study and "test" the theories over a number of years. Only then can some judgment be fairly obtained.

*To bring you these descriptions I studied and used a reference, a wonderful book by the hugely talented Theodora Lau; as mentioned above, "The Handbook of Chinese Horoscopes". This, is now co-authored by her daughter, Laura Lau, and is still available and highly recommended if you would like an insight into how the unseen forces connect with and influence our lives.

Psychology & Sociology.

Some readers may be surprised at what I am about to suggest. Some business people may smile and shout "Eureka!" The simple fact of the matter is, that many problems of interaction between people can be resolved by using this wonderful ancient method, by analysing staff, work partners, life partners or even groups that are supervised. In short, if there is trouble in the workplace, or at any gathering place, then by working out people's Chinese Horoscopes and rearranging people, all conflicts can be managed.

Example.
Some time in the late 1970's, I was running a Martial Arts class which was well attended. In it was one Full Instructor and four Trainee Instructors, all of whom were supposed to be supervising and looking after various levels of beginner to intermediate students. Then, of course, I was supervising and watching *them*. After a few weeks the tensions between them became more and more noticeable. This made me wonder why. One night I went home, got their Membership Forms out, which had their date of birth on there, and then did a quick check with Theodora Lau's book, The Handbook of Chinese Horoscopes. The issues became clear immediately! There was conflict in both Elements and Animal Signs, so I set to work. Then, on the next meet, I took my list of "compatibles" with me to the club and called all five of the five over to me before starting. I then told each "leader" which team-mates they would be working with, then set them off on the new deliberately grouped plan. It worked! The tension vanished instantly, they all did what they were supposed to do, without question, and all did it smoothly; to the delight of the students as well as myself.

How did it work?
Quite simply because of the Five Elements and the 'Control Cycle'. If, for example, you have a Supervisor who is a Water element, then they can work very well by "watering" a Wood Element junior. In other words, Water helps Wood to grow. There are of course many combinations, so going into so much detail here would be a specialist subject, and this book is merely introductory.

Summary.

The Chinese Horoscopes are highly accurate and will show you "the animal that hides in your heart". Theodora Lau's book/s, for I have bought several, have helped me decipher incompatibilities with students, relationships and, as shown above,political or other characters true natures.

On the other hand, I know another wonderful lady called Jane Sunderland, a western Astrologer and good friend. It was she who recommended me to the Astrology group to do the aforementioned lecture. Her chart making skills and consequential readings were truly divine – as in Universally connected. So it has been my pleasure to experience both the Yin and Yang of Horoscopes, as they say, up close and personal.

These methods are handed down form generation to generation, just as Theodora Lau is doing with her daughter Laura. They are not gimmicks or party novelties but real science, the science of the Universe (TAO). As we are all connected, to the Universe and each other, then hopefully, like me, you will find these tools invaluable in your quest to make sense of this Earth-walk. I strongly advise it!

"You cannot see it, but it *is* there.
You cannot touch it, but *it* touches your life.
You may get pulled in a new direction,
or drawn away from another,
simply because this is your life.
TAO is active in us all."

~ Myke ~

CHAPTER NINE

THE TAO OF FOOD AND DRINK

"We must eat to live, not live to eat."

Many people enjoy eating as a satisfying experience. It could titillate the taste-buds and leave you feeling comfortable and secure, knowing that you will not be starved that day. For some eating can be a problem, a real health hazard!

We are probably all familiar with associated food and reason disorders, like Anorexia or obesity caused through "frustration" or "boredom" eating. How many understand the problems that may be caused through eating the wrong kinds of foods? For example, too many eggs will cause a build up of cholesterol, too much "fatty" foods can create heart problems and too many sugary foods may lead to excessive weight, sugar diabetes and so-on for there are many illnesses and imbalances caused by incorrect diet. What most people are not aware of is the balance of foods. Each item may just look like a shape, texture and colour on your plate. Like most things in life, food is taken for granted as part of a hum-drum daily routine. In recent years, some connoisseurs have developed and spread their ideas on how to decorate your plate, making the meal look more attractive and taste richer or spicier. Little thought is given to the balance of Minerals and Vitamins that form such an essential part of our daily needs and determine the outcome of our health and strength.

The single biggest problem with diet is eating foods which you like the taste of; invariably sugar, fat and smoked!

The TAO provides us with all our needs, with a little help, patience and determination we can recognise all those things which are good for us and then learn how to install them into our lives in a balanced way. Harmony is again the key. Learning to mix-and-match our food is as important as learning to love the right people in the right manner. It is good to be able to love everyone, but if you associate with only those who "look tasty" then you are bound to get Mental or

Spiritual Indigestion! There must be harmony. If we eat that which disagrees with us then the internal system will try to reject it, if it is in frequent doses, illness will follow and we then need to recover, preferably by eating the right stuff. The macrobiotic books written by such great and knowledgeable authors as Chee Soo and George Oshawa tell us the facts.

Sexuality is part of the human form, just like all other animals on this planet and across the Universe. No matter how high one thinks their intelligence is, the hormones and glands will always produce the urge to have sex; denied by some, this is the *natural* animal urge to procreate. Control it, especially having babies, but do not deny it.

If a proper diet is not adhered to then problems will appear. We can see this in the Western Hemisphere as compared to the East of old. It is from the older, more deeply established Eastern cultures that we draw wisdom from today. Frigidity in women and listlessness in men are common among us today. Why? Food and drink! Women are said to be Yin, if they eat too much Yang food they become imbalanced, they will be miserable. They become more masculine and may detest the sexual desires of men and have no desire to love or be loved by men. They may also be attracted to docile, feminine men, become degrees of homosexual or devote themselves to animals, especially pets.

According to the ancient and well observed Taoist notations: A male who consumes too much Yin food will become feminine, too placid and asexual. He may loose his will to be positive, to fight the good fight, be outgoing and active; all natural Yang aspects. In modern terms, he becomes a "wimp" (derived from "Whimpering") and generally cowers from life. He may become more feminine in his ways of thinking or acting.

Note: This is the long held general view, but the author also believes that past life or family attitudes or events may also play a valid part psychologically.

A healthy man is Yang; Strong, active and centripetal. In terms of pathological extremes he may become violent, destructive and cruel.

A healthy woman is Yin; passive, soft and centrifugal. In terms of pathological extremes she may be too weak, negative, anti-social, escapist and exclusive. Too yin and she becomes psychotic and devious. The balance is always a very fine line.

The remedy may be easily discovered and utilised. The difficulty lies in keeping to a healthy regime in a world full of junk-food pollution. First you have to discover your weaknesses, then you can go to work on them. In the chapter that deals with the basics of Chinese Horoscopes you will see that each person may have five Yin/Yang stems. This, I believe, can dramatically affect a person's outlook and is a case in hand where diet may be applied to swing the balance. Take, for example, a woman that I know well. She is soft, gentle kind and intelligent. She has FOUR YIN and ONE YANG stem on her Birth Chart. Her reactions are leaning toward the pathological extremes of reclusion and escapism. The simplest remedy would be to cut out Yin foods, such as, sugary drinks ("pop" and "cola"), fruit juices and sweets, beers and dairy products. A small increase in Yang foods, like apples (in season), spices, carrots, water-cress, onions, wheat germ, brown rice and parsley, would make lots of difference.

As a Martial Arts instructor I have seen many unhealthy people enter my classes for Taoist Kung-fu or T'ai Chi Ch'uan. I have known and loved many people for their various endearing or amusing ways or quite profound characters, but so very many are or have often been ill. This kind of "ill" is not seen, physically. The "symptoms" are revealed through behaviour. The Japanese have a word for it, "Sanpaku"; imbalanced through diet. Loss of primordial sexuality, aggression, unfounded fear, escapism, and what nowadays are labelled as various Mental Health Disorders, etcetera, I've sadly seen it all so many times.

It is a fine line that we have to walk and occasionally we may veer from side to side. As long as we can recognise these "wobbles" we have a chance to rectify our state before we damage ourselves, or others! I consider myself to be one of the very lucky ones, I have balanced stems and maintain a fairly stable outlook with a "neutral" background in almost all that happens around me. But like you my friend, I have suffered the misfortunes of myself and others and the temptations of under or over-indulgence. My words of wisdom to you are "Heed The Way, for it will exist long after you."

There is a popular saying in Taoist circles, and that is "Tao provides." We try to loose all that is either unnecessary or excess to our lives, leaving a Soul that is free to expand, develop and move when and as it needs to, in whatever direction. We become more "instinctive" as we tune-in with Tao.

Yin and Yang Foods

There are some differences between Macrobiotic regimes of one Nation and another. What some regard as good or moderate, others regard as poor or bad. I can only assume that this may be for one or two reasons, 1) Climate and changes in particular food structure or personal reaction to a food, 2) Personal translations and understanding. But this is no problem. In the West we have coined-a-phrase, "grey area", in relation to Industry, mainly. But if we think of the main types of food as being either Yin or Yang, then we can take those that appear to cross as "grey". Thus, with a blending of White/Yang and Black/Yin we can either take it that it is "well balanced" or we can leave it.

The Macrobiotic (from Macros = great, bio = life) regime is a method of eating and preparing food which may enable you to function properly, with the least amount of bodily interference from sickness, ill-effects of clogging and blockage, overload and deprivation. Being imbalanced will bring about a state of disorder whereby you will become confused and lacking in confidence. Get two people together who are imbalanced and "Wham! Sock! Pow!" (See, The Tao of Love and Sex.) Balance is the key to a Macrobiotic way of life. Once you understand what is Yin and what is Yang, food can be ingested properly in proportions that are suitable for your own body.

 Macrobiotics is derived from both Chinese and Japanese cultures. The basis of Macrobiotics is the "Natural" theory. If you look at other creatures on this planet, or any other planet, you will see that they automatically balance their daily diet. Those with "pets" that are fed on unnatural things will notice "strange tendencies" in the animal's nature. For instance, a person (who may be Vegetarian) will often buy tins of Dog/Cat food at the Supermarket. The meat which is in the tins is usually extremely unnatural for that animal. How many times have you seen a cat or dog leap on a cow, bite it to death and rip out its liver, then cook it in gravy? When did you last see a dog killing a Pig for its supper, or plucking a Chicken and then cooking it? Animals hunt for food or those who do not eat flesh forage. Humans have a tendency nowadays to want to go to shops all the time, this is the "forage instinct" kicking in! However, stick him or her out in the "wilds" with no shops and say "Go provide!" And they would be lost. We have been changed by commercialism and industry, drastically.

This is not to say that we all need to don leopard skins and go hunt in the wild. Of course; you would never forgive me if I suggested that you give up all your electronic gizmos, flashy cars, wardrobes full of clothes or shoes with brand labels on the outside. What we do need to do is face the reality of it all and then change the face of consumerism. How? Simple, we just buy those things which we *need*, not *want*. That "hunter gatherer instinct" is responsible for our excesses, including all those things you buy on impulse but never use, then sell some months down the line at a car boot sale, or on the Web. This behaviour is no different to a domesticated Cat. People buy kittens because they look cute and fluffy (the maternal or paternal instinct!), Then it grows up, despite being over-fed, the cat then goes out and kills all the birds, wood mice and other creatures it can catch, just for the sake of it! It is the cat's "nature" to hunt and kill, just like it is a Human's nature to forage and gather too. This is what we have to get under control. Excess.

Over thousands of years, many wise men and women have added sayings which help us to identify the problem areas of life, from a human perspective, then make adjusting it our goal.

The Way of Life (translated by Dr Kiang, Kang-hu & Witter Bynner. Verse 12.

> The five colours blind,
> The five tones deafen,
> The five tastes cloy.
> The race, the hunt, can drive men mad
> And their booty leave them no peace.
> Therefore a sensible man
> Prefers the inner to the outer eye:
> He has his yes, - he has his no.

Traditionally, these verses use "he" or "man", but it equally relates to women as well. Women, it has been said, are "the nest builders" in a average relationship, so naturally like to have some comfort and a few decorations to make the home or "nest" feel and look nice. Even the homes of single women or lesbian couples I have seen are well decorated and have many visual or physical "comforts" in them.

At this point there are bound to be some people who accuse me of being sexist or something equally absurd. Imbalances being what they are, I would expect this. The reference above is nothing to do with sexism, being male or female, self-classified or self-labelled Non-Gender or anything else apart from a Human Animal. Humans, like all other animals, have natural instincts and that includes "nest building"! As for men, well, males generally have tendencies that they follow too.

THE BALANCED APPROACH

The Japanese term for Tao is Do (Way). Sometimes, like the Chinese, they describe its functions as "The Unique Principle" which all amounts to the same thing, Nature's Way and the Power of The Universe. The man who was probably responsible for "introducing" the West to Macrobiotics was one, George Ohsawa with his book, Zen Macrobiotics (Ignoramus Press, N.Y.). When he was asked about eating meat he replied, "Eat only those things which do not protest or run away!".

An old theory says that by eating some animals, certain aggressive characteristics were transferred to the person. We now know with the aid of medical science that when a cow is slaughtered, adrenalin is soaked into the meat, along with substances that were unheard of in old China and Japan, artificial growth inducers, antibiotics, etc.. Beef, Lamb and Pig (pork, bacon) are extremely Yin by nature, too Yin to be balanced properly, but the "added effects" may also cause untold damage.

General advice is simple;

* Eat only that which is Natural (No processed food/drink)

* If you must eat meat, make it white and organic.

* Reduce Salt intake. Use Sea-salt or a "mix". *

* Pick young, fresh vegetables and fruit for more goodness.

* Balance Potassium (YIN) and Sodium (YANG).

* Balance foods (approximately 1 part Yang to 5 parts Yin).

* Do not over-fill your stomach. Small but regular.

* Avoid late night binges if possible.

* Try to eat fruit and vegetables that are locally grown and in season.

* Blend your own juices, herbal recipes and cook them with love.

Yin and Yang Table of Daily Foods.

MOST   MOST

YIN -YANG

Meats - Sugar - fruits - dairy - nuts - vegetables - cereals - fish - eggs

(Note: there may be some exceptions to the rule in this list.)

(Coded items below)

Codes: +++ Very Yang, ++ Moderate Yang, + Lesser Yang.

Codes: - - - Very Yin, - - Moderate Yin, - Lesser Yin.

FRUITS & NUTS:

- - - Pineapple, Papaya, Mango, Grapefruit, Orange, Banana, Grapes,

     Dates, Figs, Pears, Pecans, Walnuts.

- - Apricots, Lemon, Peanuts, Cashews, Almonds, Peaches, Plums,

     Lime, Avocado.

- Coconut, Currants, Blueberries, Melon, Olive, Hazel-nut.

+++ None common.

++ Apples.

+ Chestnut, Strawberries, Cherry (sour red), Raspberries.

DAIRY FOODS:

- - - Yogurt, Cream, Cream Cheese, Butter.

- - Whole Cows Milk, Camembert.

- Gruyere, Edam, Roquefort.

+++ None common.

++ Goat's Cheese, Goat's Milk.

+ Dutch Cheese, Egg.

VEGETABLES:

- - - Artichoke, Asparagus, Bean Sprouts, Broccoli, Cucumber,
Aubergine (Egg Plant), Tomato, Yam, Potato, Mushrooms.

- - Green Peas, Red Cabbage, Rhubarb, Zucchini (Squash),
Celery, Lentil, Sweet Corn, Cauliflower, Brussels
Sprouts, Green Peppers.

- Green Cabbage, Bamboo Shoots, Chard, Chicory, Leeks,
Beetroot, Lettuce, Sprouted Wheat.

+++ Burdock Root

++ Pumpkin, Kale, Carrots, Dandelion (leaf), Lotus Root,
Water Cress.

+ Turnip, Onion, Radish, Garlic, Mustard, Ginger Root.

CEREALS:

- - - None common.

- - None common.

- Barley, Cornmeal
(de-germinated & Un-enriched), Oats, Rye (Whole Grain).

+++ None common.

++ Buckwheat.

+ Brown Rice [1], Millet, Whole Wheat, Wheat Germ.

BEANS:

- - - Soy Beans, Kidney Beans, Lima Beans, Chickpeas, Black Beans, String Beans.

- - Lentils, Split Peas.

- Adzuki Beans.

+++ None common.

++ None common.

+ None common.

DRINKS:

- - - Soft Drinks ("pop", "cola", etc,.), Tea (with dye stuff), Coffee (Caffeinated), Chocolate, Fruit Juice.

-- Wine, Beer, Soda.

- Mineral Water, Deep Well/Spring Water, Herb Tea (most).

+++ Ginseng Tea (Root or Strong Extract).

++ Mu Tea, Kuzu, Umeboshi Juice.

+ Bancha (Green) Tea, Kokoh, Chicory, Dandelion Coffee, Yannoh.

OCCASIONAL'S:

- - - Honey, Jam, Lard (Animal Fat), Vegetable Fat.

---

[1] Brown Rice is considered to be the most perfectly balanced food as it is one part Yang to five parts Yin; Short Grain being best. White rice has little nutritional value as its best assets have been removed during processing.

\- -   Vegetable Oils, Soybean Milk, Tamari.

\-   Sunflower Oil, Safflower Oil, Sesame Seeds.

+++ Seaweed, Curry Powder.

++   None common.

+   Human Milk, Bancha Tea, Miso, Sesame Oil.

Use this list to study your daily input, find out just how much good there is (or not) in ready packed and processed foods. With some modern "healthy eating, quick meals", you will have to buy a book on Additives and see what the chemical properties of E200, E420, etcetera, are! But generally, if you can prepare your own foods from good, wholesome ingredients, then you should not have any problems in maintaining a healthy body and a worry-free life.

If you really do not have the time to buy and use all fresh, local produce and resort to using tinned or prepacked, then be very careful of what you choose, mix it well with "balancing" ingredients and remember...

Psychology & Sociology.
Again, this comes into both spheres of mental health management and social behaviour. Tragically though, the problems of Mental Health caused by dietary influence may not be so easy to correct, as many stem back through the subject's parents and possibly even their parents too. The reasons for this are that food provides Vitamins, Minerals and Proteins, as well as other elements or trace elements. These are used to build cells and bones as the baby forms in mother's womb. If the right amounts are not delivered, then baby may be born with an imbalance. A classic example of this, which most people may know of, is Rickets; a condition whereby the baby did not get enough Vitamin D, which is also important in body calcium functions, and causes bone problems, the most obvious being a bowing of the legs. The word "obvious" is the most important here because many problems caused by lacking Vitamins & Minerals are not so easy to see, such as Brain disorders.

This is a vast subject. Modern Pharmaceutical Science is looking into creating drugs or Beta-Blockers to "counter" certain disorders, but not into the cure; I am sorely tempted to say "as usual" here, because this is the biggest difference between Traditional Chinese Medicine and Western Orthodox Medicine, apart from the "age gap" of a few thousand years! In TCM, every time, diagnostics is used to try to pin-point the cause. When the cause is found, then the imbalance can be treated. In Orthodox, the Symptoms are usually observed, then they look for a way of "blocking" that process; in pretty much the same way as they advise taking Pain Killers for a headache, but not finding out what caused the headache! Frustrating.

As a parent I know well the difficulties in trying to get children to eat something new, something raw, something green. This difficulty is exacerbated by the fact that children can so easily get hold of sweet things. These are habit forming, and let's face it, we all know what it is like to eat something sweet and then crave more. This problem can start with infancy and first solids. If I were a mother, switching from Breast Feeding to Artificial Milk, I would scrutinise the Contents, especially for additives, colouring and the very evil Aspartame (which turns into Wood Alcohol when warmed up in the body, and that's Formaldehyde, a toxic poison!)

My youngest began solids on Short Grain Brown Rice and Broccoli, which is a very, very good start. Somewhere down the line though, perhaps at school or elsewhere, things changed and the all too familiar "food tantrums" began. Issues followed.

Diet is a very intricate and complex subject, especially when you look beyond the normal or "obvious" levels. My feelings here are that is may be easier to change diet on a National level than on a household one. If we had genuine people in government positions, such as Minster for Health, who *actually understood* health, then we may begin to get somewhere. There are many, many additives that need to be banned (starting with Aspartame), more local produce which needs to be organic and consumed locally, more education needed on the true values of foodstuff and severely limiting the amounts of sugar, fats or seed oils used in all products.

Change is like that proverbial journey of Ten Thousand Steps, it begins with just one step. In recent years we have seen many changes to general consumer provisions, but somehow, and I feel that mainly because of *unknowledgeable* people in government positions, it all goes pear-shaped. There has been huge take-off for Soy Milk in 2020, but manufacturers are allowed to use GM Soy, which as yet, we still do not know the lab Test results for, or any long-term data on health effects. Another issue with that is that some are topped up with vitamins, minerals of even sugar. This is what they call Fortified. Sounds good, but when you consider how many other things are "fortified", how the heck are you going to keep track of your daily Vitamin and Mineral intake? You can. Literally, have too much of a good thing. For example, too much Vitamin A may also be highly toxic bringing about symptoms of headaches, drowsiness, dry and itchy skin, dry hair, swelling over the bones in the legs and arms, skin peeling, lack of appetite or even vomiting.

In the book, mentioned below, there is a wealth of information on the subjects of vitamins, minerals and all things dietary. The individual can select one thing at a time to swap in their personal diet for something better. On a larger scale, people who are supposed to be in positions of health management, would be advised to study the subject more deeply than just on an Industrial level; e.g. who can produce what, where, and how much tax do they contribute; the real question is, "Do they contribute anything towards better health?"

We need Society as a whole to be catered for in a much more natural way, not commercialised foodstuffs, polluted, contaminated with chemicals and additives, or processed until they look nothing like the real thing. Remember…

"We are what we eat."

~

If you wish to study the complete diet, then one of the other books in this series is listed here.

T'ai Chi Diet II - Ch'ang Ming.

Author: Prof. Myke Symonds

Life Force Publishing.

ISBN: 9780954293239

Available from all booksellers in almost all countries.

Feed the Body. Feed the Mind. Feed the Spirit.

It seems today, in the larger commercial countries, Governments, who are driven by bankers and Industrialists, are making people dumber, leading them astray with misinformation and generally discouraging them from thinking for themselves. In education you find fodder for the factories or offices, but no education on practical, everyday things. Food, fashions and clothing is getting more and more artificial. Nothing is real any more. Nothing, that is, except us. The mere fact that you are reading a book like this is to try to gain understanding of things, probably life, so reality seeking.

My life has been full of spiritual events since I was born, and consciously around four years of age. You may not believe some of the things I have experienced, so I shall leave them out! The point of this page is "feeding", not memoirs.

We have an animal body. That body needs food and water. The more "natural" that food and water is, the more natural and in-tune with life we shall be. Just think about chemically altered food or drink, high in sugars, artificial chemicals like Aspartame (turns into Formaldehyde when warmed up in the body!) We need more natural diets in order to function correctly, or even 90% correctly.

Oxygen is another essential ingredient of everyday life. We need clean oxygen and deeper breathing; hence Ch'i Kung/Qigong (Energy Training). Mix the oxygen with fuel and it produces power, proteins and good body function.

There is an old saying in traditional Taoist Arts, "Shen. Ch'i. Li." Shen is Spirit. Our body contains a Spirit, the real "us". It is the "driver" of this earthly vehicle. Ch'i is the energies (3 main types) which the body produces, and we can also use "outside" Ch'i too. Li is best described as Kinetics; something physical propelled. So we eat foods to fuel our body, rebuild tissues, grow, get stronger and function better. In turn we harness the powers of breathing to enhance our Spirit. The Spirit, or ID, then sits at the heart of the Control Room and operates everything. The better quality food, water and air, the better quality operations will be. Simple.

No matter how much you try to think, without a more pure diet, those "operations" will be dulled. Hence many Taoist, over many thousands of years have brought you these incredible Arts for "Long Life" and better health.

CHAPTER TEN

THE TAO of MEDICINE and HEALING

Traditional Chinese Medicine (from here on 'TCM') has so much more value than western Orthodox Medicine and Surgery, as it concentrates on education and prevention firstly, not cure; quite rightly and logically. TCM developers thought that *cure* meant treatment came too late, whereas most problems could have been avoided with a little Taoist Education, care and effort. This we can see quite clearly today as the infantile (by comparison) western medical system has become reliant on Drugs, usually full of toxic elements and bad side-effects. As illness progresses, more drugs are applied, instead of finding the root cause and correcting that!

TCM Explanation.

TCM started between 5,000 and 10,000 years ago. Western Orthodox Medicine's beginnings are attributed to the first book on the human body by a westerner, which was called 'The Book of Blood'; mainly mapping out where blood vessels were so that "surgeons" in the field did not cut through them by mistake! This was written in the 18th century. This makes orthodox medicine's history span a mere 200 years. It is still taking baby steps. Where it once relied on surgery and bandages or cauterising of bad wounds, it now relies mainly on strong drugs (artificially made) and surgery. Not much has changed.

TCM has some roots in humans observing animal behaviours when the were ill. When animals have aches, itches or sore points, they may rub themselves against a tree or rock, thus activating or suppressing Acupoints. If internally upset, they will seek out and eat the right herbs, natural vegetation. Animals also stretch their body and limbs, thus keeping the circulation good and muscles or tendons flexible; which also may massage internal organs, so helping them to work better. This is how exercises such as yoga were developed, by copying our animal colleagues. Later on, such activities were developed to a higher level by Taoist Sages, often medical experts, people who understood the workings of the body. TCM was developed step-by-step over hundreds, then thousands of years. Today it is still flourishing, both in rural China and around the world, and is the choice of many people who seek either Natural Remedies or who have had bad experiences with western Orthodox Medicine; often referred to in China as "Wai shan gei por", meaning based on external, physical aspects, dissecting and looking. TCM is based on the whole person, body, mind and spirit (Qi), and takes into account how one element effects another, one organ has an effect on another, the mind also has an effect on the body, as does food, living or working environment and everything else we do. That amounts to a huge difference between the two branches of medicine!

Perhaps I need to use an example of diagnostics to clarify my apparent enthusiasm for TCM. Let us make it a simple one. You will also see how the philosophy of Taoism is used to describe certain conditions.

A man who does not smoke cigarettes, starts to develop a regular cough. His GP sees him and thinks the man may have a Flu virus, such as the Covid Strains which affect the lungs. The family doctor then prescribes that the man goes home, isolates, and takes some cough medicine to ease the coughing; this usually contains substances such as Opiates or other strong drugs. The man takes this, stays off work, but after a month does not feel better. In fact he feels worse. His face becomes pale, his lungs weaker and his cough worse. The family doctor may then prescribe pain killers or anti-inflammatory tablets, plus some sort of tranquilliser for the man's growing mental stress and discomfort. These drugs all have side-effects, and if mixed badly with another, can have deadly effects.

A similar man who does not smoke, develops a regular cough. He is concerned about his health, so goes to visit a TCM practitioner. The TCM Practitioner asks the man many questions about his lifestyle, whether he smokes, works with chemicals, sprays, or has much dust in his house or workplace. He will also enquire whether the man is happy in his general life. In fact, a complete "picture" will be built up of the man's lifestyle. The TCM Practitioner will then need to go away and study the answers the man has given, perhaps after having tested his pulses (plural) and also taking note of his skin colour, eyes, tongue and other tell-tale aspects of the body. The next day or soon after, the TCM Practitioner may ask the man to come back and talk to him again. He may ask,, for example, "Are you unhappy about something or under great pressure , perhaps feeling stressed?" If the man has not smoked, does not work with farm, factory or other chemicals, and is in a clean atmosphere, he may say "Well, yes. I do feel stressed actually." This may be because of relationships; i.e. nagging or constant dissatisfaction. It may be because of his unhappiness with the type of work he does, and not feeling fulfilled. Stress (a mental state) can cause physical illness, which first shows in the skin (the body's largest Organ) and then can manifest via the Lungs, which when weakened can become infected, causing coughing.

In terms of diagnosis, the questions about lifestyle, diet, family, etcetera, are all crucial, as there is a need to pinpoint the cause of the problem, not just identify the symptoms. The TCM Practitioner may then recommend herbal drinks to reinforce the lungs and skin or to induce calmness. He/she may also recommend a change of diet, lifestyle, perhaps even work, depending on what seems to be causing the unhappiness and resulting stress; as stress is the outcome of dis-ease, or being ill-at-ease or unhappy with a recurring situation.

TCM uses the Wu Hsing or Five Elements in relationship to the body and its main functions and organs. The Heart or Emotions are labelled under Fire. The skin and Lungs, Metal. Fire controls or destroys Metal. In this case, it is used to describe the effects of the emotions (heart) affecting the Lungs (tissue). There are both positive or supportive cycles of the Wu Hsing and negative or destructive cycles, like the example of Heart Fire affecting Lung Metal.

The Taoist philosophy, as previously stated, has been used successfully in this way and many others for thousands of years. TCM has been developed for many thousands of years. Why would you only treat one part of a body, or even remove that part, when in fact something else made that part ill? This is the case with Cancer. Sadly, all too frequently. Cancer cells are present within all of us, within all creatures. Cancer cells are kept "in check" by healthy tissue, immune system and a natural or wholesome diet and exercise. Once the diet becomes poor, or exercise stops, chemicals enter the body, then the cancer cells can burst into life, a negative life, whereby they start to "feed" off the other weak parts of the body. If a person is diagnosed as having cancer early enough, that person could have a change of diet, begin new exercises and even take natural herbs to fight that cancer. I have witnessed this, so many times, and I am truly saddened that when someone submits themselves to western orthodox medicine, they are subjected to long waits, unhealthy drugs and the cancer cells are left to grow until they are big enough to see easily, perhaps then being cut out. But cutting these diseased cells out, most times, causes fragments to enter the blood stream and move to other parts of the weakened body where they multiply and destroy even more. Time is of the essence. The main causing factor of Cancer is bad health; includes poor diet and lifestyle.

TCM has a different approach. STOP anything form taking hold. This is called Preventative Medicine and is simply "lifestyle and diet". However, if someone does slip. And most of us humans do, then simple, natural treatments are available and have been used, tested and proven over the annals of time. Here I have to add another possible human "weakness", that of wanting to try something new over that of something old and well established.

To many people the medicinal and healing skills are something which is done by 'professionals', that is people who do it for a living. Say this to a Traditional Chinese Martial Arts Teacher and he/she will give you an inscrutably quizzical look. In days of past, it was probably a long way from the village to the nearest doctor and then you had to have the money, and most had not. The local "Ch'uan-shu Kung-fu" teacher was usually widely experienced in treating cuts, bruises and bone-setting. He probably had some good knowledge of other matters, too, things like diet, stress and, of course, therapeutic exercise. There were some who were just concerned with fighting, but there were many who helped discover some of the most important medical breakthroughs and facts.

The Yellow Emperor.

The Yellow Emperor, Huang Ti, was not only reputedly responsible for the initiation of the Taoist philosophies, but was renown for many other things including Martial Arts practice and development, and of course, the 'Huang Ti Nei Ching Su Wen' - The Yellow Emperor's Classic of Internal Medicine. Although the oldest known document in Chinese Medicine, it was not translated and published until 1949. It caused quite a stir and has been responsible for a dramatic revival of traditional medicine in China and elsewhere. A translation by Ilza

Veith was published in the United States of America, it alone triggered numerous medical studies and revelations.

There are many branches to the tree of medicine and healing, some go this way, some go that way, but one must remember that they all come from the trunk, by far the widest part and with very deep reaching roots. When you are looking at medicine you are looking at a very big tree!

My old Taoist Master, when asked about type of healing method, said, "There are many methods. The Chinese have a list, low on that list are drugs, higher is acupuncture, above that is Herbs, exercise and diet..." At the top of the list is something which may be well described by the immortal phrase, 'Physician, heal thyself'. For to keep illness and imbalance at bay is far more important than curing it later!

(He was right, he always was. After all, it was he that looked at a pregnant woman and predicted a baby girl. He was right again!) That amazing man was Grand-master Clifford Chee Soo, probably the most remarkable man I have ever met in my life. He ran a free clinic in Edgware Road, Paddington, London, called The 'Hoi Mar Brocade', at 377 Edgware Road in Paddington. The shop was lent to him as a favour from a very grateful man whom he had healed.

There, in his "spare" time (as if he had any!) he treated over two thousand patients with varying problems. Some were recommended to him by "Specialist" Doctors of Western Medicine who could find no symptoms of any problem, let alone a cure. He treated them with words, herbs, exercise and massage/acupressure, for this he charged nothing.

One very astonished woman had this to say about his health practises, "*I was amazed that he didn't charge, he told us he gets pleasure from seeing people get well. I was living on tablets, nerve pills and everything, I was told I had had anaemia. I haven't taken anything since I started coming.*" She continues, "*I've had migraine since I was a teenager. When I heard about Cliff I was rather sceptical to think that one man could achieve what modern medicine can't. I did feel the difference after a few days, but wouldn't let myself believe it! Then, after a while, my daughter told me how much better I looked. It's not just mind over matter, the cure runs into months and you couldn't fool yourself that long. To me it's like a fairy tale. He,s done for me what Doctors can't."* (Luton & Dunstable Evening News.)

This kind of reaction is not uncommon as Doctors in the British NHS system, as with Doctors in other countries, are only educated in Orthodox Medicine and Drugs, or Surgery, not "Corrective Medicine", as is the case with TCM. TCM, Traditional Chinese Medicine, is still practised today, but by very few in the West. Then, not for free! Traditionally in olden China there were very few medical practitioners around, so the local Martial Arts Instructor was often called upon to help with injuries or health problems as, traditionally, he or she would learn about the anatomy, injuries and healing methods alongside Martial Art skills. This begat a saying about the line of development from student to Master, noting three main stages that the person would go through: "Warrior. Healer. Priest."

In old China there used to be, what I think, a very sensible and practical system of professional help. When a Doctor became qualified to practice s/he would start out helping or sharing a practice. As he became more proficient and saved lives or cured illness, then his reputation would spread and s/he had more "credits". When a Doctor moved and opened a practice of their own, lanterns would be hung outside the door. One large lantern for every life saved and one small lantern for every serious illness cured. You would choose your Doctor by the amount of lanterns and availability. The best of it is that you paid your physician a weekly fee, but only whilst you were well and in good spirits. If you became ill then the money would stop until you were healed again! What a marvellous incentive, a pity that that system does not happen here in the west.

Instead we are plagued by huge pharmaceutical companies, who all have different incentives, goals and morals (most appear to have none!), And who, as this book is being written, have been responsible for 16,000,000 deaths to date world wide *at least*, from what they call "Gene Therapy" (Therapy means "treatment" not healing!) And was then called Covid-19 Vaccine. Experts are saying that those who have not been killed by the Protein Spikes causing Thrombosis (Blood Clots) or Heart attacks after weakening the walls of the Aorta

Artery, etc., etc., have had their DNA tampered with, and many young people may not be able to produce children. (Search Doctors4CovidEthics)This stops here, as the list of known effects is far, far too long to write here and this is not the right place. To conclude, all I shall say is that this has been highly unnatural as well as highly suspicious, but not dealt with by any country's legal system; as yet, although complaint and legal charges have been laid with the International Criminal Court of The Hague.

Again, commercialism has attracted many of the worst kind of people, those who only care about profits. The old beasts who used to be referred to as the "Mad Scientist" are still there, still creating drugs and chemical concoctions that kill people, too often in a slow and painful way. Many of these "Big Pharma's" have been fined £$Billions, time after time, for killing and injuring people with their experimental drugs and jabs, yet they have not been arrested, or shut down! Why?

In countries that participated in what is now widely called "The Scam-Demic" or "Plan-Demic", we have seen a takeover of leading country's medical systems. Doctors are told what to do, or risk losing their licence; thus resulting an many Doctors injecting their patients with a pseudo-vaccine that creates artificial spikes, then caused problems with blood clots, weakened heart arteries, birth processes and much, much more besides. This, I do not have to tell you, is not "healing" people. The 45,000 people per annum in UK alone who die from prescribed drugs is not "healing", it is the exact opposite! Why? Money... money, and more money. All of these Doctors and Nurses, and others who have delivered the lethal doses, should be struck off the Register and jailed. Dress it up any way you like, but behind the fine clothes, white jackets and fancy offices, is Manslaughter.

Why Are So Many Leaving?
It seems that many people are now leaving the National health services and are going solo, learning to look after their health better. Hooray! But, the big question is, "Are they doing it properly?" In UK, the NHS has crated delays, much paperwork, more delays and then more paperwork and delays, so getting to see someone takes an awful long time. As you know, any imbalance needs to be addressed as soon as it is detected, not six months or five years down the line, by which time it has got worse and become something much harder to fix. We need to loose Commerce and reinstate Care.

Tao & Healing.

So, what of TAO, how does it relate to healing? We have already looked at Food, Drink and Exercise (Love and Sex nearly always follows). Here I would like to take you on a quick tour of the body as seen by Practitioners of The Way. It is a very excellent system of diagnosis and therapy which uses all the aspects of Yin/Yang and Wu Hsing (Five Elements). No doubt most folks have heard of Acupuncture by now. This uses needles to stimulate the flow of bio-energy (Ch'i, Qi, Ki or Prana) around invisible pathways in the body called Meridians. Ch'i, it has been proven, does exist and has three main elements; Infra Red Micro-waves, Static Electricity and Electromagnetic energy. Does this mean that you will be forcefully attracted to a metal object, give yourself a nasty shock and cook your dinner at the same time? I don't think so! I like to use analogical expressions to relate with. In this instance I use the motor-car system.

The car is an obvious method of transport, so is our body. Your Mind operates the vehicle/s. To make the transport run you need fuel, for you, food and drink, for your car, petrol - at least I hope you get it right, otherwise I'm not going to stand near you if you are Cremated! Your fuel is transmuted into a more useful substance by your stomach. It is turned into a fuel cocktail of vitamins and minerals and is transported to other parts of your anatomy. Your heart pumps around the blood and carries oxygen from the lungs around the body. The two substances are mixed, the "burn off" produces energy which drives the muscles. In your car the petrol is mixed with oxygen in the carburettor, this is pumped into a cylinder, compressed and ignited by a spark which causes a small explosion. This energy is transmitted, by cams and cogs (organs, blood and nerves), to the wheels (Muscles) which propel your vehicle. See, it is simple... or is it?

Your car uses electricity for many things, most importantly, the ignition. If this fails we say, "It's dead!", but unlike our body, the car can be revived. The lights, signals, horn and sometimes windows, radio, roof and heater are all worked with the wonders of Electricity. It has to be carried by Meridians, call them wires, if you like. At various points along those wires there may switches, relays, delays and gizmos - I like the gizmos, personally. What happens when your little car does not feel well? You call a car-doctor, a mechanic. He prods and pokes its various bits and pronounces that you have not been looking after it too well. What have you been doing to it, driving it hard and neglecting its little circuits! This has caused a severe breech, a point where the energy can not continue in order to do its job. So he cleans it up, brushes away the erosion and checks that the "contact" is being made properly again. A turn of the key and your little eyes light up with glee as you have visions of going "Brrrumm, Vrrrummm," all the way home, your favourite cassette of the veggie Rock band "Nutloaf: Bat Out Of Hell !" playing merrily and warning pedestrians of your rapidly approaching presence so that they may run for their lives! How thoughtful.

The Meridians in your body are all related to various organs or functions. There are two main channels which are very important, the Governing vessel - Tu Mei and the Conception Vessel - Jen Mei. Then there is the Heart Constrictor - Hsin, Pao Le Ching and the rest which all relate to Organs rather than functions, except the most important, The Triple Heaters - San Chao Ching. The others are; Lungs - Fei Ching, Large Intestine - Ch'ang Ching, Stomach - Wei Ching, Heart - Hsin Ching, Small Intestine - Hsiao Ch'ang Ching, Bladder - P'ang Kuang Ching, Kidneys - Shen Ching, Gallbladder - Tan Ching and Liver - Kan Ching.

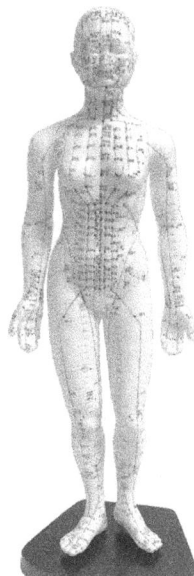

Some Meridians begin at the Feet or Hands. Some flow upwards (Yin/Centripetal) and some flow downwards (Yang/Centrifugal). All of the Meridians are shown below and are represented along their paths by dotted lines.

In Acupuncture or Professional TCM, the appearance of the body's state, symptoms or ch'i flow all use terms that are based on the Taoist philosophy and then defining medical terms; e.g. "fluttering", or "Cold", "Lazy" or "knotty", referring to the activity of a Pulse or Ch'i flow at specific points. So again we see the way that the philosophy of Tao has gained widespread use and importance in many fields of living.

Each Meridian has a purpose and serves a function associated with the vital organs, but not necessarily for that organ. Each organ functions at a peak during certain times of the day. The chart below shows the peak time as well as the stem (there are five Yin and five Yang viscera), organ and flow of ch'i.

(P.E.L. = Peak Energy Levels)

P.E.L.	STEM	ORGAN/FUNCTION	FLOW
1 to 3 am	Yin	Liver	Centripetal
3 to 5 am	Yin	Lungs	Centrifugal
5 to 7 am	Yang	Lge. Intestine	Centripetal
7 to 9 am	Yang	Stomach	Centrifugal
9 to 11 am	Yin	Spleen/Pancreas	Centripetal
11 am to 1 pm	Yin	Heart	Centrifugal
1 to 3 pm	Yang	Sm. Intestine	Centripetal
3 to 5 pm	Yang	Bladder	Centrifugal
5 to 7 pm	Yin	Kidneys	Centripetal
7 to 9 pm	Yin	Heart Constrictor	Centrifugal
9 to 11 pm	Yang	Triple Heater	Centripetal
11 pm to 1 am	Yang	Gallbladder	Centrifugal

Conception Vessel - Yin - Centripetal

Governing Vessel - Yang - Centripetal

When a person becomes ill, there will be imbalances in the flow of bio-energy along one, or more, of the Meridians. At various stages along the lines are points that are actually small "boosters". Because the energy is only mild, it looses momentum. Therefore it needs to be boosted along the line, much the same way as a TV signal has to be on very big buildings. A person who is studied in the Chinese methods of Diagnostics and Healing will be able to tell, after questioning and examination, what the problem/s may be. Treatment can be had in several ways, acupuncture, Acupressure, herbs, massage, diet, exercise, counselling or some alternative method. There is no "best", it is purely horses-for-courses.

One of the forms that acupuncture or Acupressure uses is the Five Element theory (Wu Hsing). This roughly dictates that if, for example, an illness or imbalance is related to the Element of Metal (Lungs: Skin, muscle, hair,etc,.), then Fire (Heart: Emotions, energy, etc,.) was possibly the cause. Earth stimulates metal and water controls fire. The patient would get whatever was the best treatment according to the exact condition. It is not easy to describe the full workings of ch'i and the combinations of Yin/Yang/Five Elements here. So, like the car electrics, the patient's "circuits" are "cleaned up" and made to flow properly again.

Amongst the many aspects of diagnosis are the translations of physical appearances into elementary diagnostics. These include the shape of the body, skin texture, elasticity and colour, the appearance of the tongue, eyes, hair, finger nails and stools. It is all part and parcel of the same thing, holistic health practice, known to some Chinese (and others) for over a thousand years..

There is enough material within these pages to satisfy your curiosity and give you something to study. Another reason not to go into too many details here is that it is a very vast subject. Not only that, I do not wish to encourage anyone to "experiment" with various points as this may likely lead to a disruption or imbalance which can cause illness. And that is not at all the purpose of this little book! But I am sure that by now you must be getting the idea that the philosophy of TAO and in particular the Yin/Yang values used to describe the two basic harmonious forces, is indeed a valuable one. It is one which can really help you to put your life, problems and even your state of mind and health into an easy to view perspective.

Note: One of the best methods of avoiding possible illness is to take up some sort of (properly taught) Chinese exercise, like Ch'uan-shu Kung-fu, T'ai Chi Ch'uan or Pa T'uan Chin. The Eight Strands of Silk Brocade and T'ai Chi Ch'uan are by far the most popular among Chinese - and they form one-quarter of the world's population.

Ch'uan-shu Kung-fu is extremely good for those who can bear the demands of the more vigorous exercises, but it is an excellent way of keeping fit and supple as well as a dynamic means of self-defence. Add to this a healthy and balanced diet and you have the makings of a stronger internal system, better resistance to disease and a longer, happier life.

A class taking Tai Chi for Health led by the author.

TCM Values.

How TCM compares to modern Orthodox Medicine is like trying to compare an apple to a brick.

Let us look at the basics of diagnosis first. If you go to a modern GP and say "I have a stomach upset." Usually they will assume that you have either caught a stomach residing bug, or have eaten something to upset you, perhaps getting Salmonella from reheated meat. They will then offer you a prescription of some drugs that will supposedly settle the stomach and reduce discomfort. The actual "cause" has not been established in any depth.

Go to a TCM practitioner and they will ask how long it has been, were you sick, what was that like, what have you eaten or drank in the past few days and lots of other very pertinent questions. This is to try to establish what the actual *cause* was. Once the cause has been established, then the Practitioner can advise on how the patient can treat it; e.g. what to eat, drink or avoid. The practitioner may also use some Acupoints on the Stomach or other Meridians which will ease pain and discomfort. No unhealthy residues of drugs would be left in the body.

Where, for example, inability to have children may be the problem, a TCM Practitioner would seek to understand family history, diet, lifestyle and even work or living environments to try and determine the cause of the problem. Readers may be surprised to know that many health problems are caused through imbalanced diet, unhealthy lifestyles or environments, or even "stagnation" within the body. This is where TCM strives to recognise all factors concerned and then apply corrective measures, which may include dietary changes or additions, exercises like Qigong, or even some hands on massage and manipulation techniques. You try getting hands-on massage or acupressure when you strain a muscle or have other body aches from a western GP - even Physiotherapists avoid most contact now and it takes anything from three months to a year to get an appointment, by which time you could be healed, or dead.

As stated before though, the main aspect of TCM is in the *preventative* field of medicine. You may ask, "Is it *medicine*?" Yes, it is. Many foods are a type of medicine that we eat, or should eat, and each type of foodstuff we eat has different values or properties. If we eat too many Yin foods, like potatoes, then we will create a swing toward poor health and overall function. At the same time, we can "overdose" on vitamins; something my youngest finds very amusing! Most people may think that vitamins are good, therefore the more you eat, the better off you will be. No. This is why there are guidelines for daily recommendations; If you look on food packet or tin labels, you should see something like RDA, Daily Amounts, Daily Recommendations, etcetera. This may say of the content, for example, "Calcium - 200 mg - 25%", meaning this is 25% of the amount your body needs daily. If, again for example, we have too much Vitamin A, then we can cause problems as the body cannot deal with that much. Too much Calcium may cause problems too, such as Kidney Stones if we do not have enough Vitamin D with our daily amounts also. This is all dealt with in the book T'ai chi Diet II - Ch'ang Ming.

One of the problems which besets the western world or "richer countries", is that food producers are allowed to add Vitamins and Minerals to products such as breakfast cereals, soy milk and even children's snacks. This can cause health imbalances, se beware!

Mental health imbalances can, I repeat, also be caused by an excess or lack of different types of foods. It is a complex situation, but can be addressed with a bit of knowledge, awareness and practice. To do so requires the knowledge such as in the above mentioned book. That book also has a Special Needs section, which sadly is growing! In the days of the past, in China, there were no "special needs", just those with and those without food. The basic principle of Traditional Chinese Diet is that when dinner was served up there would be the Staple (Rice) and then The Five Flavours. The eater would then rely on his or her body's instincts to choose which complimentary flavours of food they wanted to keep in balance. This may seem like a very strange concept and even unimaginable to many in the western world, so let me make an analogy.

A pregnant woman will often have what they call "cravings" for different foods. This may be foods with more calcium in, vitamin D or whatever, but she will just want more Milk, biscuits, or whatever, without even knowing what is in them. This is her body using its survival of the fittest instinct to to try to supply her growing baby with what it needs.

Disaster! The western world has industries with no knowledge of food health, morals or cares, that advertise chocolate, sweet sugary things and chemical additives which will all dull the Mother to be's senses and natural body instincts! Hence many parents to be have imbalanced bodies and mothers create imbalanced babies, or babies with health issues already when born.

This all reflects on society and behaviour.

Is it mum to blame? No, unless she has already studied diet and health then ignored it. It is Industry and Government. They are both centred on "profit" and usually overlook the real issues of health and fitness. Profit comes first, poor health follows, then a breakdown of society through different levels of health and awareness. That is when the Government steps in and tries to implement laws that will change things, not what they should do, which is to look seriously at what is causing the problems, food and lifestyle.

Pretty much all the Psychiatrists and Psychologists I have ever met are concerned with one thing. That is the thought process; is it *wrong*, if so how can we label it and how can we adjust it by suggesting behavioural changes, or by trying strong drugs that suppress emotions, or feelings. This again, is like sweeping the muck under the carpet. One day there will be a huge bump under that carpet that will be a trip hazard, so to speak. Of course, some may claim success, that their patients are walking around in a bit of a daze, but not doing what they did before. Realistically, the damage can be so deep, so engrained in the body that it cannot be repaired that easily. All serious repairs take serious time. The issue here though, lest we forget, is that of Diet and Lifestyle, every single time.

It may not be possible to correct all imbalances within a year, ten years or even a lifetime, but at the same time, we really need a new generation of dedicated professionals who will look at TCM, diet and lifestyle, and then start training people to make these changes today; not through some lame, hands tied government department, where petty bureaucratic paper shuffling takes ten or twenty years. We need change now. We need that change in schools, where young people will grow up to expect to raise children[1] and be useful members of a progressive, well balanced society.

Almost everyone, including myself, groans when politics is mentioned these days. Wee must, really must, tackle this issue head on though, just like we must tackle our own personal diet and lifestyle. It is the politicians who are ruining the world. They are not in it for our future but for their own, or their spoilt offspring's futures. Therefore we need healthy, intelligent, honest and sincere people who can *change* the face of politics. Change it for the good, that is.

- Get rid of processed foods and artificial additives.

- Take licence away from firms making unhealthy products

- Encourage seasonal food eating, balance, nutrition and health through preventative measures; including exercise and Qigong.

- Reconfigure the NHS or Public Health Services, to include more Preventative measures, like diet and exercise. This would, of course, mean less reliance and control of the "Big Pharma", who

---

[1] That is, if there are enough intelligent and healthy young people who will live long enough or be able to reproduce after the pseudo-vax injections that have already killed at least 16,000,000 people, old and young, world-wide.

really push their drugs with "incentives" for government ministers and doctors. This means a massive change to…

- Encourage Farmers to grow healthier crops; cut out Rape, for example, and use more Organic methods. (Oh, big killer chemical industries will hate me! ;-))

- Add to GP or Doctor training to include full diagnosis of diet and lifestyle, recognition of physical features that are telltale health indicators, more questions about diet and lifestyle asked, then more of a "hands on" approach; such as massage and manipulation of injured muscles or joints and ability to prescribe exercises the patient can do himself.

- Training within the health services for all staff, so that they may make themselves healthier, more well balanced people, before they attempt to help others.

- Changes also need to be made to employment and conditions, so that staff can participate at the start of every day with a simple, qigong based, exercise class, and also be encouraged to eat a healthy breakfast before coming to work (likewise with school students), so that they may have the body and brain power to tackle their day. Breaks should be health focused too. A happier healthier workforce will make for a better production line as well as a better community.

- Make the world a Ch'ang Ming zone, where everyone eats more natural, unprocessed, healthier foods that are in season, so benefiting overall health.

- Birth Control. This was already mentioned, but needs to be listed here. The Earth cannot support and endless number of people[1]. Women, especially, as they are the child bearers and egg makers, must consider the world first. Do not have children unless you can afford to care for them until they are working adults. Or if there is no or little prospects for their futures.

---

[1] From 2018 to today, we have seen a plan which, although denied, has wiped out over 16,000,000 people from the population. Many more may have been labelled as "Natural causes". This is part of an undeniable plan to drastically reduce the Earth's Population to a more manageable level. And although there may be more sinister intent behind the plan, the fact remains that there are afar too many people on the planet who cannot be supported.

- Interracial harmony and respect. No religion or belief should ever get in the way of harmony and progress. Everyone left on Earth needs to work together to implement these changes. Anyone not doing so is just holding back progress and future development, and creates unsustainable wars and conflicts which do no good whatsoever.

- Finally, although you may think of more, the most basic thing which needs to be changed in all members of the human races, and that is "Self". The notion of self-importance, selfish wealth hoarding or general selfishness is the cause of many problems. We need to eat, we need to live, but we need to learn to work alongside others, like many Teams already do.

Only when we can change these things can we hope to progress. That needs to start right now with Politics and changes to how the internal processes work (e.g. Whips and bullying or exclusion, bribes, incentives, etc.) and changes to the voting systems too; I have always said and will until I move on from this body, that we need Coalition, not single Party Governments who are self-centred.

It is my hope that this chapter alone may surprise some readers. It may need to be read again and absorbed more. However surprising or strange it may sound, it is a fact that issues arise from imbalances in people; be they a politician, factory worker, school child or parent. These imbalances are in the main created by diet and lifestyle.

I fully understand if you bought this book because you are seeking to change yourself, or you are studying Tao and Taoism, or you are interested in Psychology, Sociology or philosophy in general. You are of course correct, if you thought of making better changes to yourself, your lifestyle and thinking. It is the only place to start, of course. Every journey of thousand miles begins with just one step.

Whilst changes can be made to you, the individual, this is not enough. It is too little, too late. Changes can only be made at a National level that will reshape a country's future, and that must be with thousands of people, not just a few.

As a footnote, raised to mid-page prominence, so that it will be seen, I would add this.

Some, to whom this kind of good, or better new world organising, may pose a threat to their financial or power position. This may lead to accusations and character assassinations of the author saying that his thinking is "too radical" or "not at all feasible", etc,. This would be expected, as this is the kind of sickness of mind that was spoken of earlier in the book. It has been the way of those who are power grabbers for many centuries, and in Twenty-first Century world orders we can see that clearly. To-boot, I am not seeking power or wealth, am near the end of this "Earth walk", and profits from books like this are so small and few-and-far-between, that money spent on maintaining it is likely to outweigh any small profits; over 50% of which are made by retailers, and another hefty chunk by Printer/Publishers! The morals and reasons behind this book are from a Taoist perspective, which is to observe, digest, understand and then translate the subject. Then to help others; we all have to live together, so let us make it better.

Clarification.
It is known from years of experience with supposed quotes, speed reading and other anomalies of reading lines and mistranslation, that many people do get it wrong all the time. Media groups like Facebook are a classic example of this. Someone reads a story or sentence then accuses the author of meaning something else. For example, in the context of diet and health, I might write, "Whatever happens to you is just LIFE." A reader might then translate that as "It's life, just get on with it!"

When I talk about diet, mental and physical health issues in this book, I am not saying "Change your diet tomorrow and you'll feel better." Of course, it simply does not work like that. You may feel better over time, if you stop eating whatever is making you ill. But all things take time. The list, overleaf, is an example of that which needs to be done on a global scale, changing many individuals, then they will change their offspring, and if those children follow the same guidelines, they will not only have a healthier future but will also improve the health of their own offspring.

That old Confucius saying, about righteousness in the home then spreading to the world, works the same way for health. Start with one person, influence another and another, then so it spreads. Not possible? Yes, it is. Look at how Veganism spread, very rapidly across Europe, UK and USA, probably other countries too; which I have seen no reports of.

Clarity also needs to be made about food and psychology. If, for example, someone has been diagnosed as a Schizoid Paranoiac, then changing the basic foods on his or her plate is not going to undo any damage overnight. It might have some effect, over time; no medical tests have been done to this regard, that is diet and mental health.

What I am suggesting in this book is the connections between food, exercise and the way we behave. Having had students with varying degrees of mental and/or physical health problems, I have witnessed the changes in them, before training, as they commence training, then after some year or more of training, including making changes to diet and lifestyle in other ways.

One man was a drug user, got into fights and drank more than "enough" alcohol. In six to ten months he gave up smoking, gave up drugs, cut beers down to a "pleasant couple", and changed in his entire outlook… except for fighting, but he became a fully trained and registered Doorman instead, so at least doing it for a good cause!

The old gentleman with Cancer has already been mentioned, earlier in this book. He could have stayed cured. He skipped the essentials,

My Old Master who had helped so many people, including those with "incurable disease" (according to the National Health Service).

In the Diet book you will find other examples, like the pregnant woman and bananas.

There have been many, many instances of people changing, both in physical health and mental health, and for the better. TCM is, as one would expect after 5,000 to 10,000 years of constant development, a truly wonderful thing. In the early days of study though, even I was tempted to say "No! Can't be. Too simple!" But simple it is. Powerful it is. Ignored it should not be.

Hopefully, by now, dear reader, you will be getting the notion that the world can be changed, but only if we start by going backwards, just a little, to our more natural ways that our Grandfathers and Grandmothers used to practice, untainted local foods, grown organically, eaten in season and cooked from fresh. What the Supermarkets do on a National scale, could be improved to take in a more localised operation. Likewise, Farmers, many of whom have created Farm Market Shops, could do similar, supplying ready to eat daily meals for those who are too busy with work to prepare them themselves.

If anyone has a garden, then I can highly recommend growing a few vegetables to help out with the household budget, but more importantly, get all that lovely fresh taste, more vitamins (which start dying off the moment a plant is harvested, so the longer the process, the less helpful!) And Minerals from organically treated soil. Quick note: It is possible to grow vegetables organically with borders of Herbs that will help keep pests away, but at the same time attract pollinators. Seek information on successful organic vegetable growing.

Awareness.

Hopefully, instead of "speed reading" or "mistranslating" anything which is written in this book, readers will study each chapter, take time, and see the links between subjects. They are not tenuous, they are solid and easily provable by scientific tests; e.g. a group of people with 'x' ailment are split in two two parts. One does Qigong, the other does no exercise at all, but just sits around doing jigsaw puzzles. Then improvements in 'x' condition are measured by professionals.

In Korea, Harvard Medical University, and other more forward thinking places, they have already performed such tests with T'ai Chi for Health, and found significant improvements amongst those with common ailments such as High Blood Pressure, Arthritis, Cancer, balance issues and more.

Just imagine, if ten readers of this book in every mainstream country in the world, say Ten, then taught ten students (110 people involved) corrective exercises and better diet, then those ten "took it home" and influenced just two members of their family (330 people involved)… and so on. The results would continue to multiply, each one person becoming a good influence on many others.

Then, if we could achieve what is in that list three pages back, wow!

CHAPTER ELEVEN

The TAO of Love and Sex

"They want to love one another but they don't know how"

Sandor Ferenzi

The Yin and Yang of sex and relationships is a very complex one for it relies upon the frail and often volatile human weaknesses, such as emotions. Emotions are or can be a storehouse of past experiences (Yin) and can suddenly pop or explode (Yang) under pressure. In terms of interaction with a partner this can produce some very stressful effects on any relationship, no matter what age or preference. To help me in this chapter I have looked for some "classic" examples or cases and a few quotes from well known authors plus a few of my own observations; which I hope are well balanced and without bias. This is what I strive for, balance and truth. Sometimes, if the truth touches the nerve of a person in whom the emotions can be volatile and unstable; the truth may cause an outburst. These problems I constantly wrestle with, as I do not wish to upset any person, but the truth as I see it has to be reflected in Nature (Tao) as a whole, and there are many things that humans do that are not natural. To not care about doing something which upsets another human is not right, therefor if someone upsets me unjustly I will say something to the effect of asking them why they did that, or, if I feel that they are mentally numb then just move on and hope that one day, they will realise their mistakes; you cannot help someone who is blind to the fact they need help or simply so off-the-wall that they refuse to accept that they are ill. Illness is Disease, and as mentioned before, that breaks down to "dis-ease" or "ill at at ease", meaning that someone is feeling uncomfortable, is irritated by something being not right or a few other translations. Let us not waste time on the pedantries of meanings as these are often seen differently by individuals. When you are physically ill your body feels wrong.

When you are mentally ill the whole of your life feels wrong. In both cases you may not understand the reasons "Why?" In a relationship that is not working it will be almost impossible for either partner to ascertain why it is not working as they think it should be. That is where a good Counsellor should be used to mediate. The worst thing would be to seek the advice of one's friends, who may also be imbalanced!

The Driving Force.

Sexuality, is usually the physical attraction of opposite sexes, and procreation is the basis of life itself. It is the key to existence, without it Life would simply cease to exist and love is the flowering of sexuality. To love is to live. Yet sexuality, whilst being the attraction that starts a relationship often, is also the basis for the breakdown of many relationships at a later date. Sex is literally driving millions of humans insane and destroying families as well as killing hundreds of thousands more each year with sexually transmitted diseases.

We are seeing the erosion of the sexual polarity (1990's), women are becoming more masculine and men are becoming more feminine. Forward to 2010 and men wanted to grow full beard while women followed fashions with pop stars and skimpy clothing and a full-time "flirt" mode. Underlying though, all the time, was confusion about sexuality and relationship values.

Because of many factors, men and women now face huge relationship issues, and that is before they get together. If this erosion continues the result could end the Human Race, at best it creates misery and suffering through the illness which the imbalance creates. It was said by Sakurazawa Nyoiti, in his book about macrobiotics, that, "In a country like the United States, where a huge majority of the people suffer from chronic illness of one kind or another, it is no wonder that sexual maladjustment is the rule, rather than the exception. No wonder there are so many broken marriages, so many divorces, so many desertions, so many illegitimate births, so much agony caused by abnormal sex practices."

This was written in the mid-nineteen-seventies, now we are in 2022, and it seems very apparent that the U.K. and the rest of Europe has more than its share of the same illness: Since this was first written we have seen in the UK an acceptance almost of the de-sexing to a point where it becomes almost fashionable; I witness much underlying confusion and discontentment which normally shows itself as stress and illness; There is also a growing disregard and numb acceptance for others as we have Big Issue magazine sellers vying for space in the streets with charities trying to get you to sign Standing Orders for payments of £250 per year; some other people *pretend* to be homeless and beg for money, maybe using puppies to get extra Social Security payments and "soft touch" animal loving victims to give them money, which mainly is spent on drugs, as their faces give testimony to; one of my students entered the training hall early (in 2002) and was first there (entering through two sets of doors, up a short flight of stairs and into a large hall where he placed his kit on the opposite side from the door), he decided to go for a pee and came out to find an unknown man going through his bags. This man had just followed him in off the streets, but on finding out that the 'student' was there to participate in a Kung-fu class left abruptly! And Norwich used to be such a quiet city. This is all a reflection of an unhappy and very dishevelled society.

Liberation or Destruction?

Society has a problem, it is feminism, masculinity and sex. There was a movement in the sixties from single sex classes in schools to mixed sex groups. This, say some psychologists, caused boys to act like or mimic girls and girls to act like boys. Many teachers had noted a decrease in learning levels because of the apparent "over-interest" in the child's opposites. In my mother's day it was said, "men were men and women were women" (Little did she know about what went on behind closed doors!). Things did not always necessarily run smoothly. In recent times we have seen yet another feminist movement. Whilst I am in every way supportive of women *and* men being liberated from some of the double standards and degradations of society, I am totally appalled at the apparently large percentage of mentally imbalanced (but seemingly "normal" on the surface) people who prey on those who are going through a phase of instability in their life. Let me risk quote from my own personal experience;

At a neighbour's party one evening I was talking to a young woman about her job seeking. I knew that this woman was a lesbian, as were many of her friends. She told me that she had applied for a job within the Social Services, to work at a home for young girls who, in the main, had been sexually abused or assaulted by male relatives or friends, etcetera. She then expressed glee at the prospect of having "...so many opportunities get [her] hands on some fresh young girls" and introduce them to [her] ways!" I can only say that I find this as sick and appalling an attitude as those despicable males who allegedly assaulted the girls in the first place. There have been many, many cases of police officers having child pornography on their computers, and Priests or local Councillors being involved in child abuse. How much of this goes on? How many victims are there in these sort of "care" situations are not aware of what the underlying motives and reasons are? Why are such jobs in Social Services and schools, prisons and other institutes apparently open to such mentally sick people?

These are not just my views or opinions. My mind is partially a reflection of most people's thought or knowledge, I pick up their ideas or science based facts as a whole and then translate them into analytically blended paragraphs. There is much unrest in the world with both sexes. Here is an odd thing I have noticed: Men generally mate by instinct. This is a very animalistic practice, governed by chemicals, hormones and visual stimulation, mainly. They group as other animals do, quite often the males go off to share sport or other male interests. They say of their females, "Women! Who understands them?"

Women choose their men and mate in a similar animalistic way, but there are many more chemical and hormonal processes going on inside them and they are generally looking for a good provider (Hunter/Gatherer). They too like to go off and group with other females and share interests, not so much sports traditionally but more often babies, houses, fashions, other people's relationships and who's doing what with whom. They will often say of their males, "Men! Who understands them?"

(These are "generalisations, of course, as no one statement fits all.)

Most men will complain that in longer term relationships women try to change men's habits and ways, this causes rifts. Many men also feel that women use "entrapment" to seduce him into a relationship by wearing sexier clothes or make-up that give off sexual signals. After the person is "procured" the clothing changes; except when she goes out with friends to a club. He also falls into the habit of not dressing up for his partner and they take each other for granted. This does not happen in what may be termed "a natural relationship", because couples are attracted by 'internal' things rather than external. Mature and balanced people will realise that sex is just a method of procreation for making babies. Recreational sex is not natural, it is another form of distraction. This is not to say that we will stop wanting sex with our partner. Healthy people do want sex, but not crave for it all the time, that is an imbalance.

Someone should do a huge survey about sex and relationships. They would find that sexually active couples fall into two categories, the first the young and single. The second category would be those in relationships of varying time spans. This would then be sub-divided into other categories of sexual activity and other factors. For example: In a relationship where one partner was fit and physically clean and attractive but the other was fat and did not look after their appearance, then loving sex or cuddles would be missing most of the time. In a relationship where both were fit, healthy and relatively stress free, then sex and cuddles would be far more prominent and the "twice a week" statement would be the norm (desiring sex more than twice a week may indicate the "Chinese Take away" syndrome and not feeling satisfied for long after. Good sex should leave you feeling good for at least a couple of days and glowing with love for your partner). However other factors can take their toll of your sex life, like having babies or toddlers around (demanding and tiring), or too much work and money worries, et cetera. The government creates a demanding and stressful society and the sheer density of population concentrates those stresses, or problem areas, into towns and cities where there is little room to escape and people allow their stresses to be unleashed on strangers; road rage, pedestrian rage, ill mannered people in shops, et cetera.

So, what is the problem. The problem is the way things are done, the confusion, too many cooks spoiling the broth. The TAO teaches us that by looking inside ourselves we will learn. Not outside to magazines and fashionable minority trends. Feminism and Masculinity have to go. False images (fashion and make-up) will only confuse the senses and cause further problems. We must open our eyes, minds and hearts to what is natural. Be yourself. Just look at some of the problems caused by imbalance.

It seems that whilst some females nowadays have been going about experimenting with their powers, men, generally those who wish for a monogamous and steady relationship, have become confused and bewildered as a result. You have to look deeply, not just at the surface as many people say they do not want relationships simply because they are fed up with meeting so many undecided, cheating 'players' or mind changing partners; often confused through reading magazines, talking to friends or watching crap TV shows!

Many more long term relationships have been broken up by people who have become confused, unhappy or otherwise bewildered by a sudden onset of apparently blinding choices that are seemingly open to them. I have seen with my own eyes and heard of with my own ears the troubles and traumas caused by our new, so called, Liberated Age. The temptations are often too great for weak-willed women, or men, who are suddenly "head-over-heels" with a simple smile from a comparative stranger; of who knows what background. Men who did nothing but work hard and care for their wives and children, suddenly out of a marriage and home for no other reason than their spouses overnight desire to "try something new" (one of the pathetically ill thought out sayings that may be bandied about by groups of women in discussion, especially when one says, "I feel trapped or bored..."; what happened to putting an effort into relationships, faithfulness, commitment, or being a two-sided affair?). They did nothing wrong in particular, for they were just being themselves - sometimes adversely affected by imbalanced diet or social habits. Women, who may likewise be confused, who are preyed on by a Lesbian female who delights in having such powers of 'sympathy' that she can sometimes take a woman away from a normal relationship with a caring male. Men/women who have inherited the "screw them all and leave them flat!" approach; promoted by those sick and imbalanced people who have long fallen from the wayside. Sex without genuine caring is nothing but masturbation using a partner.

There are some women who call themselves independent, but still rely on a man to check their car or do ordinary household repairs. There are some men who will blindly agree with anything a supposedly liberated 'Ms' will say so as not to appear to be ignorant, or sometimes just to get into favour for the possibility of sex/company; I see this in mixed company quite frequently. Men who will prey on women who are drunk, or women who are postnatal depressed and not getting on too well with their husbands (a natural kick-back as they subconsciously blame their spouse for giving them the baby that keeps them awake at night or cries during the day for more attention). Women who think it is all right to strip naked and jump into bed with a man, cuddle, kiss and hold each other closely, indulge in foreplay and then say "no!"; This sounds feasible in theory, but some basic understanding of the Human Species is left out... we are just animals with natural animal instincts and chemical/hormonal reactions! We are flesh and blood, but we have minds that are flexible and that appear to be capable of more choice than most other creatures.

Our body consists of flesh, bone, water, energy and various organs, glands, etcetera. What these foolishly naive people do not understand is that when a man and a woman come into close proximity (dancing, cuddling, touching, etcetera) certain things happen within the body. In the woman there are chemical and hormonal productions and releases which, unknowing to the owner, produce sexual attractant odours. Kissing is the Human-animal's form of "bonding". (Kissing produces semiochemicals from the sebaceous glands in the sides of the mouth and edges of the lips. These are very strong sexual stimulants.) Likewise in the male, sexual attractants and stimulants are produced (the armpits are one of the strongest pheromone sites and nearest to the female refractory organs). But it is only here that the real trouble begins, for there is a far stronger physical sex drive in the male, once aroused he feels this strong sub-conscious urge to fertilise "his mate", whoever she may be at the time! (I say this because a man is highly aroused by intimate contact and his hormonal/chemical drive often hits Warp 7 - as in Scottie pronouncing, "Och! The ship can'ne handle it Captain, it's shaking to bits!"). Mind you, there are quite a few women like that as well, "hold on tightly, it's going to be one hell of a ride!". Such relationships could be classified amongst the Extreme Sports category for their proximity to explosive dangers... or even back injuries.

She, on the other hand, has a confusing and bewildering at times physiological/emotional play going on. She wants to mate (physiologically), but (psychologically) is it with this man? Would she have his baby? Confusion between the two can understandably set in and cause dispute. There is a need for change in viewpoints here as well as an understanding of human nature. Meanwhile, he is driven by his in built urge to procreate while she dithers and changes her attitude more often than she changes her knickers.

There is, again, a simple answer to the problem. The Natural Way of Relationships. Getting to know someone for themselves, not just for sex as a pastime or "fun" - a scene given too great a momentum by contraception. There may be moments in your life when you want someone for comfort and the feeling is mutual, or you feel the need for more than just the mental support of a friend, but I am talking about people who flit all the time and Serial Adulterers.

Develop natural attraction through a healthy body and mind, not make-up. Learn to appreciate Nature and each other for what you feel, not what you subscribe to. Teach the children to consider all, not use and abuse all.

Are your eyes wide open?

There are many contributory factors to the decline in society nowadays, advertising that promises "ideals", encouraged escapism into romantic fiction and much more, all leading to confusion and lack of sustained interest and efforts. One of the biggest problems nowadays is Contraception. Its general use has been seen as an excuse to get straight down to the nitty-gritty and "bonk" freely with anyone who takes your fancy! It is usually a short-lived physical pleasure, I am told, and can be a long lived mental pain; as deep in our hearts we are looking to be loved and wanted sincerely. Having sex is a very intimate experience, so being dumped afterwards can have traumatic effects subconsciously. To coin the phrase of the "stoned" and unwary sixties, "free love" is not all that it is cracked up to be. Without the courtship and bonding rituals that make one feel secure and loved (cared for) in a long term relationship then there will be no lasting happiness. We have to satisfy our deepest sub-conscious level, that which Freud called "the id", that we are happy with our partner over a long period of time. Unfortunately, there are too many people putting negative thoughts into relationships these days, like some of the examples above. People who have not studied The Way of Life and are mentally, sexually and deeply confused about "what is right".

Traditionally, both with other animals as well as the Human-animal, mating was a slow and deliberate play. He, on feeling an attraction, would strut his stuff. She would choose a man that might fit the bill. If the two get closer and become acquainted, then they first find out about each other's likes and dislikes. If they get on well then they will start to go out and about a lot more frequently. When the time feels right (not just when they feel randy or frustrated) they may gently caress and have some physical contact - slowly getting used to each other's bodies, odours and 'feel' (intuitive). The sexual organs may be the last parts to be touched.

Because the Human animal is capable of various levels of intellect, there arise problems. These problems occur mainly due to peer group and media pressures or influence. Quite often there is confusion about what is really desired. The easiest trap to fall into is that of accepting the heightened excitement of having sex with someone new (discovery of the unknown) as an excuse not to face facts and accept the responsibility for sorting out longer term relationship problems! Many of these problems nowadays seem to relate to work, family, plus first dates experiences. Get real! You are never going to have as much time for each other when kids come along, so do not expect it. Work has to be done to pay the Bills. Try to organise your togetherness time around each other's schedules, not just one persons. Being "a pair" means that two people are involved, therefore sitting down and working out what is possible with any spare time should be a joint operation. Children do need a lot of looking after, especially when younger. When older, they need more looking out for to keep them safe and on the right path. As for First Date thrills, well, I'm afraid that you may have to take your head out of the thrill-seekers clouds and get real on that one too. There is certainly no reason why you should not have fun - and that is why Date Nights have become so popular - but is never going to be the same as that first couple of months of discovery. Perhaps learning to appreciate what you have, instead of whining about what you used to have, might make long-term relationships better?

TV is not helping, is it. It is fully loaded with dating shows now. If that makes you long to have that adventure again, then maybe you were not ready to get settled into a relationship in the first place. Many a rush decision has been based on Hormone reactions. It can be so hard to resist those natural hormones and attractions, but this is something we must learn to do if we want to avoid heartbreak and unhappiness in the future. There are lots of very upset and unstable children in the world who see their parents split-up because someone said "It just isn't working any more!" What effect does that have on kids? Maybe "Oh, relationships do not work, so let's just have sex and move on"?

When sex does take place between a man and a woman, there is a way of enjoying and enhancing the sexual energy, one I personally believe more natural, desirable and enjoyable for both partners (if both actively give as well as receive). This is for the male and female to enjoy prolonged foreplay. In this way the sexual energy is aroused, heightened and built up, the energy channels (Meridians, the energy paths treated in acupuncture) are opened and full enjoyment may be experienced without inhibition, fear of failure or frustration (much of this may be alleviated by having a compatible partner and the security it brings). During orgasm (not ejaculation), often simultaneous or close, each draws from the other's energy and the woman benefits the male's Yang energy and he from the female's Yin energy. A full, healthy and enjoyable relationship between the two partners can then continue for as long as they are interested in their mutual pleasure. The ch'i (intrinsic energy) is increased and the meridians opened curing many ills (often 'tension' related). Of course, with guidance the Taoist Sexual Control Exercises could be practised if so desired, but not necessary.

I remember that as a healthy young man with a positive appetite for sex, the type of girl who was more than willing to jump into bed with me too quickly worried me. Being teenagers it was natural to try and get the girl aroused, but more often than not if she said "yes" within a fortnight I was disappointed. In those days we were warned about V.D., Syphilis and Gonorrhoea, the tales were horrifying! In this day and age it horrifies me even more. When we succumb to the charms of another we are taking a risk, from AIDS and other Venereal Diseases (which many ignore for purely selfish and fleeting moments of orgasm), from Psychological Trauma and future unhappiness and insecurity bred through past mistakes. No wonder that we are now seeing a World-wide revision in moral ethics. It can not come soon enough. Directly and indirectly, we have all been or are being affected. It is time to consider the real pleasure and security of a long-term relationship with someone who you feel really good being with. Taoism teaches us a better way.

Some Customs Hold Moral Philosophies.

In Japan an old tradition takes place on the seventh evening of the seventh month of each year. All young girls and mature women who seek love write love poems on little pieces of flimsy paper. These come in seven colours and are attached to bamboo poles outside of the houses, rich or poor. The paper is carried off by the evening breeze, hopefully to the stars. The seven colours connote the seven words which describe the seven kinds of love, these are (as near as translation allows); Blind Love, Sensual Love, Sentimental Love, Intellectual Love, Social Love, Ideological Love and Universal Love. Of all these only the last, Universal Love, seems free from Mind only or body only bias. It is only with Universal Love that the World can be put to rights. Through having a healthy partnership one becomes well, happy and complete. This brings feelings of peace and contentment as well as a more benevolent attitude toward others, as we say, "spreading a little sunshine". This way we may have only one life partner, but we can love everything and everyone.

Societies of the Far East are in fact feministic, despite any outward appearances. They are based on the biological and physiological superiority of the woman. As Sakurazawa Nyoiti says, "The Mother is the creator; the father the destroyer. Man is the warrior, woman the peacemaker." He goes on to state that most of the unhappiness and suffering in family life or relationships stems from sexual difficulties. Barely one couple in a thousand find real pleasure and so many suffer from everything from frigidity, impotence, lack of enjoyment or its opposite, too much pathological activity. With many who can not find enjoyment and satisfaction in sexual love, their lives become disharmonious and they become engrossed in finding compensatory pleasures for their other senses, like devotion to a pet, or over-eating, drinking heavily, indulge in Romantic Fiction and so on. What is the cause of all this suffering? Lack of knowledge, understanding and corrective practice, knowing The TAO.

For a more full understanding of the Yin female and the Yang male, you can refer to the chapter on The TAO of Food and Drink. But what of the problems of relationship? Women, I am sure many will not have failed to notice, might have times thought that men were frightened of them. Not physically afraid but in the sense of shying away, sexually and mentally. Why should this be? Let me use a, rather bluntly phrased quote by the famous feminist, Erica Jong, from her book, 'Fear Of Flying':

"... but the big problem was how to make your feminism jibe with your unappeasable hunger for male bodies. It wasn't easy. Besides, the older you got, the clearer it became that men were basically terrified of women. Some secretly, some openly. What could be more poignant than a liberated woman eye to eye with a limp prick? All of history's greatest issues paled by comparison" She continues later, " That was the basic inequity which could never be righted: not that the male had a wonderful added attraction called a penis, but that the female had a wonderful all-weather cunt. Neither storm nor sleet, nor dark of night could faze it. It was always there, always ready. Quite terrifying, when you think about it. No wonder men hated women. No wonder they invented the myth of female inadequacy."

Erica Jong was correct when she said that, "All of history's greatest issues paled by comparison", but she was very irrational and gave up hope a little too soon by adding "... which could never be righted."

The Taoists had the answer thousands of years ago and even now, many Taoists and some lucky non-Taoists are applying the principles to their relationships. Ms Jong was unfortunate enough not to have come across someone (male or female) who could have answered part of her problem (if she had an "*unappeasable* hunger for male bodies", then it seems she had a much deeper psychological problem, an illness). What is the answer? The answer here the same as the problem, female satisfaction. As simple as that. Although I do not know Ms Jong, it has been my dubious pleasure to meet some women like her and to listen to their comments regarding their sexual encounters. Many are brief encounters and happen when they are either drunk or otherwise "passing through" somewhere. In all of these unsatisfactory cases the thrills have been in the brief encounter, not the sex. The sex was usually hurried or the usual preconceived format; he thinks he has to do this, she thinks she has to do that, et cetera. The sex is lacking in both spontaneity and the real desire to give each other pleasure.

It is true that the average female is less inclined to reach any type of climax before the male. Because the penis is usually so sensitive to the woman's tight vagina, male ejaculation and orgasm can be reached very quickly, the more sensitive, the quicker. Even in your fifties and way beyond you should be able to enjoy "natural" and raunchy sex the fast way, but with an added experience that was not possible as a young man: providing you take exercise regularly. Also, with the good exercise of Ch'uan-shu and Qi-gong, et cetera, the penis gets harder and more sensitive now than ever before; general exercises of Gongfu strengthens the heart and metabolic system, while a healthy heart pumps blood easier and Arts like Taijiquan make you more relaxed and able to enjoy the natural flow of a sexual encounter: Until I was in my forties I never knew what a male orgasm was; What a waste youth is on the young! Women can enjoy the benefits of such exercises too of course, a firmer and more sensitive body and tighter vagina will almost certainly increase her pleasures as well as his.

Where does the answer to all our sexual and emotional problems rest? The answer lies with both the male and the female, not just one. remember, Tao is balanced. With proper understanding of the situation and willingness to help each other and cooperate, all of these unnecessary sufferings can be banished and life can be lived in full and healthy spirit, as it should. So helping each other is the key, not just expecting from each other as seems to be the case with so many misguided souls nowadays.

Ignorance is the seed of contempt and disorder. Why should it be necessary for a woman/man to have to visit several partners in a search for sexual fulfilment? I know of many who do and none who are satisfied! (Often this is due more to a Neurosis rooted in past experience than physical lack.) Some may meet someone who knows how to give a certain amount of pleasure, but it is not something which they feel they can, or would like to, maintain on a regular basis, because that would make them insecure (they would have to question their id, contact their past and face their phobias). The love that they have to offer is as shallow as it is plainly physical. Although this type of relationship can offer a certain amount of pleasure, it is only a "stop gap" at best, a momentary orgasm and/or release of tension. It can offer no peace of mind and no long term contentment, the reassurance that one has when you know that you do not have to worry about where your next lover is coming from, or what he/she might carry: As we know, AIDS is rife, spreading still and it would not be unlikely that someone told an untruth about a blood test or past lover just because their "lust" was stronger than their sense of duty and respect and condoms are no safety guarantee at all ! One has to be very, very sure of a prospective partner indeed before having sex with them. If it something that either makes a habit of then the risk factor is higher, although people can lie and the "apparent" one off may be fatal. If we must have sexual encounters or even "comfort sex" on rare occasions then some simple guidelines should be followed; does either person frequent night clubs? Is either person bisexual or homosexual? Does either use hard drugs or associate with drug users? If the answer to any of these is "yes" then there is a definite risk, if the answer to more than one is affirmative there is a far greater risk.

Please do not get me wrong on this. I am not trying to make out that I am an angel or that I know it all. No one is perfect. We all have needs and desires and sometimes we need to fulfil our desires; that is Nature. Care should be taken not to hurt ourselves, not to hurt our partners or prospective partners and also not to spread destructive diseases or social tendencies through careless behaviour. Life, and its qualities, is the responsibility of the living. That is you and me. I have also learned to put my money where my mouth is, as the old saying goes. Having been through painful divorces and other situations, which were very damaging to both myself and my children, I learned to sit back and *think*. Using experience, logic, observation and common sense, all laced together with knowledge of compatibly and other elements found within this book, I have avoided many "would be" problematic relationships, even faced with a very attractive and much younger woman, with "baby-doll eyes" looking at me and saying "I really love you Myke!" Knowing that she was already married with children helped, of course; plus few others very similar. While her insatiable appetite may not have been stopped, at least I stayed clear of trouble and bad feelings for the sake of an hour of physical pleasure. Despite not having been close to a woman for fifteen years, to date, I would much rather have it that way than get into something with another unsettled, or otherwise with mental health issues, fly-by-night. The values of a real compatibility and harmony are of far higher value than just physical appearance or sexual prowess.

The moral of this chapter is true compatibility, the ability to communicate properly with each other, to consider each other's feeling and any potential children too. Being "grown up" and talking responsibility for your actions. Not having a hundred excuses not to take responsibility. Which is better, a few months of hot sex, or many years of companionship, problem sharing and always having support?

The TAO of Harmony.

When man is Yang and woman is Yin, there can be great harmony in their lives. Obviously, attainment of this harmony is dependent on a well suited couple in the first place. Even in Japan, with its strong religions and traditions, there are special Buddhist Temples called "En Kiri". Women who have cruel or unsuitable husbands can go there to break marital ties (hopefully this works for men with cruel wives, too).

It is a blessing indeed to find a partner with whom you are comfortable and well matched. In my life I have known and loved many women (I'm not talking about sex here), I respected every one of them for who they were, but alas I can not say that many, especially younger women, were pleasing to be with for long and this reflects on both after a time. This is partly due to inexperience on both parts, if neither knows then disharmony will sooner or later show itself. Thankfully I came across Indian, Tibetan, Japanese and Chinese Arts. Meditations, Psychology, T'ai Chi Ch'uan, Kung-fu and philosophic concepts. The good fortune of this is that it has led me to TAO. With a little luck in meeting the right match, an open heart and effort on both parts, the love of a man and a woman shared can be a rich and rewarding , lasting experience which can lead to a long and relaxing life in pleasant harmony. However, we must remember that sex is not the most important part of a relationship, teamwork is; the ability to work together, for each other and care for each other.

It is with a certain amount of sadness that I witness all that goes on around me within the world, this country and the city in which I live. I see all the people that I know, or not, struggling in futility to correct their lives with 'fashionable' solutions, ever drifting away from TAO. From those who hide behind delicate screens to those who are so ill and destroyed that they inflict their bent will on others. There now so many mediators, relationship gurus (Agony Aunts) and television shows offering guidance that it has become confusing to the limits. Who offers real guidance? Where is there a profound truth? Nature (TAO) has the answers. In the Yellow Emperor's Classic, his (mainly female) advisors studied and proclaimed:

The Young and Young Partners.

Sex Guidance the Taoist Way. The only problem with the young is their natural enthusiasm to go boldly on and ignore advice coupled to a lack of experience and knowledge. One day they reach old age or maturity and realise what the Tao has to offer. But for many it is then too late. No one even begins to reach maturity until after twenty-five. Twenty-five to thirty is the age of unease, at thirty one should settle and mature in outlook, because forty and fifty are just around the corner. Young people should talk to their Grandparents or other "worldly" older folk.

When the young discover sex with a partner that they like, they will soon become worn out, disharmony follows. The young woman is quick to become lubricated and the young man is quick to erection, but he is also quick to ejaculate. This is where the problems begin. He becomes tired and worn out, but he can see that she is still not satisfied. He becomes anxious, even withdrawn from her. Lack of communication follows and a pitiful breakdown of the relationship which should never happen. If only they knew and both practised the loving ways of the Tao.

There follows an example of Taoist wisdom which I hope will be of benefit to many couples who read this little book. It may at least prove satisfying to try if you are in a good relationship.

A Thousand Loving Thrusts.

The Emperor Huang Ti had four advisors of the Tao. Only one was male, the other three women. His chief female advisor was Su Nü. A dialogue, purportedly between the Emperor and Su Nü over two thousand years ago, about the 'Five Signs Of Female Satisfaction', goes like this:

Emperor Huang Ti: "How does a man observe his woman's satisfaction?"

Su Nü: "There are five signs, five desires and ten indications. A man should observe these signs and react accordingly. The five signs are: (after foreplay)

1) Her face is flushing red and her ears are hot (red). This indicates the thoughts of making love are active in her mind. The man can now start coition gently in a teasing manner, enter slowly and thrust very shallowly and watch for further reactions.

2) Her nose is sweaty and her nipples become hard. This signifies that the fire of her lust is somewhat heightened. The Jade Peak (penis) can now go in to the depth of the "Valley's Proper" (four inches) but not much deeper than that. The man should wait for her lust to intensify before going in deeper.

3) When her voice is lowered and sounds as though her throat is dry and hoarse, her lust has intensified. Her eyes are closed, her tongue sticks out and she pants audibly. That is the time that the man's stalk of jade can go in and out freely. The communion is now gradually reaching an ecstatic stage.

4) Her "Red Ball" (vulva) is richly lubricated and her fire of lust is nearing its peak and each thrust causes the lubricant to overflow. Lightly his jade peak touches the Valley of "Water Chestnut Teeth" (depth: two inches). And then he can use the thrusting method of one left, one right, one slow and one quick, or any other method, freely.

5) When her "Golden Lotus" (feet) stick up in the manner of hugging the man, her fire and lust have now reached their peak. She wraps her legs around his waist and her two hands hold his shoulders and back. Her tongue remains sticking out. These are the signs that the man should now thrust deeper into the "Valley Of The Deep Chamber" (six inches). Such deep thrusts will make her ecstatically satisfied throughout her whole body."

[The Taoist concept states that if a man retains his Ching (sperm) by not ejaculating then he will be refreshed and able to make love again - if his penis is not aching - (although delayed orgasm and mutual climax can also be very satisfactory and refreshing, also more natural). The more he and his woman enjoy the benefits of satisfactory love-making, the happier, healthier and more youthful they will both feel. [But, it must be a joint effort, "it takes two to Tango!" See notes on next page also.]

Tsai Nü: (One of Huang Ti's three female advisors) "It is generally supposed that a man derives great pleasure from ejaculation. But when he learns the Tao he will emit less and less, will not his pleasure also diminish?"

P'eng Tsu: (Huang Ti's Senior Tao Advisor) "Far from it. After ejaculation a man is tired, his ears are buzzing, his eyes heavy and he longs for sleep. He is thirsty and his limbs are inert and stiff. In ejaculation he experiences a brief second of sensation but long hours of weariness as a result[1] . And that is certainly not true pleasure. On the other hand, if a man reduces and regulates his ejaculation to an absolute minimum, his body will be strengthened and his vision and hearing improved. Although the man seems to have denied himself an ejaculatory sensation at times, his love for his woman will greatly increase. It is as if he could never have enough of her. And this is the true lasting pleasure, is it not?"

Although in the initial stages the man may have difficulty in controlling himself, his partner can offer her help, it would be worth it in time. Sun S'su-Mo, the most prominent physician of the T'ang (A.D. 618-906) period, had this to say in his 'Priceless Recipe': "When a man squanders his semen, he will be sick and if he carelessly exhausts his semen he will die. And for a man this is the most important point to remember."

(The Tao of Love & Sex encourages men to have pleasure without ejaculating and therefore retaining their energy.)

---

[1]   Author's note; It does not affect everyone the same; thank heavens! Also, we know know that the male body needs the minerals Zinc and Selenium for sperm production. We loose it so easily after ejaculation but replace it with difficulty. This could also effect our energy levels and certainly effects the strength of the immune system. Taoist sages of old would not have been able to know this.

There are of course other parts to this study of human nature and its relationships. The team studied many relationships from all over China to discover the how, what why and when of relationships. Leaving no stone unturned they proclaimed:

May and September Relationships.
(One younger and one older partner)

These are very acceptable and quite in order.

An older woman can benefit from the younger man and he from her also. The younger man who is quick to excitement may be guided by the experienced woman. If she has had children and her vagina is not as tight as that of a younger woman, then he may not be so quick to ejaculate. He might also feel more secure with her paternal ways. She may be more easily aroused by his firmness and eagerness. This type of relationship used to be frowned upon, but it is perfectly natural and healthy for those who are single.

A younger woman can also be very content with an older man. She may feel more secure with a man who has experienced life and has a more knowing and a settling approach. The older man may be slower to reach erection (Ed. depending on, nervousness, fitness and attraction), but her tight vagina would stimulate him and her firm body arouse his desires. Being slower to ejaculate (Ed. this also depends on circumstances and foreplay) she would receive more satisfaction. She may also be comforted in knowing that as she grew older, he would be older than her still and still derive much pleasure from her youthfulness. A man or woman of the same age may desire the company of a younger partner at some point.

This society that we live in needs to be made aware of the facts that have been known to those who study the Tao for over two-thousand years. The way to a better world starts at home, with wholesome love, lasting pleasure and sharing - not just taking but giving as well, giving of oneself. Without love the world will die and Humans will destroy themselves in futile attempts at trying to find other distractions whilst becoming slowly, but surely, de-sexed and desensitised.

Blissful Union

According to ancient principles: Once a man has acquired the ability
to regulate his ejaculation he will reap the rewards, says the Nei Jing.
His vital essence will be conserved and he will enjoy love-making
with his woman much more often and to a greater degree of entire
satisfaction. Neither she or he will have to be so concerned about
contraceptive devices, pregnancy or failure to please (Ed. not so
careful in those days, eh?). He will benefit from her Yin essence and
she from his Yang essence. They will be able to make love as often
as they want and are able. Peace of mind and harmony will follow,
the true harmony of Yin (female) and Yang (male).

This is one Taoist theory. However, for fit men and women there is
another option. Prolonged foreplay can lead to a heightened
enjoyment for both partners. When the woman is ready for her man
then he can enter her and they may enjoy a mutual (or close) climax
whereby they seemingly "fuse" into one and their energy is
recharged. This may not happen every time and needs practice, even
then, each time may be different. But sexual desire between partners
is not always of a regular need or stimulus, on some occasions a
cuddle may be in order, on others a raunchy five minutes to let-off
steam, maybe something a little more stimulating, daring or exciting
like sex outdoors, and on other occasions a romantic and passionate
evening in warm environs may be the requirement. The mood varies.
This is one thing that can cause dissatisfaction and couples must
agree on a happy balance that suits both partners. Maybe he wants
to enjoy a relaxing evening by the fire whilst she wants him to smack
her bottom and be bawdy. Why not enjoy the latter, followed by the
former? Teamwork. Relationships mean that you should relate
(communicate) to each other. Even stressed and busy couples with
children buzzing around can enjoy quickies as long as there is
genuine affection between them and they are aware and supportive.

There is also the male orgasm. Not the ejaculation but a deep and
vibrant charge of energies which can cause one to convulse with
sheer pleasure. It is almost like having a small electrical current pass
through your body and make the muscles quiver, flex and spasm with
sheer delight. Why should women be the only ones to enjoy orgasms.
Men can be so wrapped up in what women want that he can forget

his own pleasure and become too tense. This can make relationships less stimulating or sparky.

There you have it. The Yin's and Yang's of sexual relationships. many people nowadays feel that they have discovered something new in their sexuality, or new ways to have relationships. The truth is though that this "age" is no different to any other, except for more media coverage and things like the Internet; so we hear about it more. Whether it is three in a bed, homosexuality or bondage, it has all been around for almost as long as humans have. What we need to consider are the facts:

- Is it unnatural?

- Does it abuse or hurt anyone?

- Can it have a negative effect on society?

If the answer to any of the above is affirmative then the simple reply is "don't do it".

In Taoist philosophy there are sexual exercises which male and female couples can practice and enjoy. It is sometimes the (less spoken of) case that there are female and female, but these need not be written as they already know what each other desire. In all, this little chapter just serves to stimulate the mind and introduce some Taoist thinking.

What must be remembered is that sex is about procreation (making babies) and is an animal instinct. As we get older that instinct may fade a little and by the time most people have reached their thirties they have matured and these instincts - and the hormones which drive them - have become lessened. By the time most women are forty they have little desire for sex, apart from feeling the need to be wanted or attractive in a physical sense. Most men think about it but rarely do it, because they are too stressed at work or are simply not eating the right foods to keep it up.

In your fifties you can still like and enjoy sex, more than once a week, but it may depend on many things; diet, fitness, stimulation; it is no good if you are looking at someone who is physically unattractive, or someone who thinks you should perform at the drop of a hat just because they are in the mood. Remember Charlie Chaplin? He was making his wife pregnant when he was ninety and was responsible for many babies; mind you, whether he stayed at home and looked after them is a matter of question.

Meanwhile, as my old Taoist Arts Master used to say, "Practice makes almost perfect." (Sorry Lao Bah, did you just mean in T'ai Chi Ch'uan practice?)

Summary.
this chapter was initially written quite some years ago, probably in the 1980's to 1990's. It has been edited now and, surprisingly or not, still seems to fit the modern world and address many of the problems in relationships.

When we get older, many things are clearer, usually in retrospect. This is where book writing, knowledge sharing and education come into play. Is there enough emphasis on how to work in a partnership in modern schools? From what I have heard, there is quite a lot about sexuality and accepting people's choices, but not enough about finding the right partner, avoiding hormonal rushes or learning to communicate.

Parents who understand these things may do well to sit down, overcome any awkward feelings, then discuss these matters. Discussions may save potential failures and despair.

So far, the book has covered the psychology and social implications of the Taoist Philosophy, or Philosophy of Tao. Perhaps now we should add this philosophy to relationship education, and not just for children.

CHAPTER TWELVE

THE PHILOSOPHY of TAO TODAY

" A person living is yielding and receptive.

  Dying, they are rigid and inflexible.

  All things, the grass and the trees,

    Living, they yielding and fragile;

    Dying, they are dry and withered.

  Thus those who are firm and inflexible

    Are in harmony with dying.

  Those who remain yielding and receptive

    Are in harmony with living.

Therefore, an inflexible strategy will not triumph;

  An inflexible tree may be blown over.

  The position of the inflexible will descend;

  The position of the yielding and receptive will ascend."

Translation: Tao Te Ching (Verse 76)

The Taoists past and present have always closely observed Nature. They/we study the effects of the plants, weather, animals and people. By their observations, and by using the philosophy, they were able to closely see that those things that were unyielding (to Nature) became "lost" from the Natural Order of things. This leads to decay and death. They observed that those people who remained free from ritual, religion, set ways and ideas, old trauma, bad childhood experiences, belief and behaviour were always more happy, healthy and content. They led their lives with peace in their hearts and in harmony with Nature (The Way). Whilst those who are rigid, set in their ways and ideas, have debauched and greedy desires, search for intellectual answers, hold on to grief or do not forgive and do not pay heed to Nature came to an untimely demise.

It is like the ruler who leads by force, those who cause suffering are soon deposed. The ruler who leads by setting his people free, will be followed and upheld. Hold yourself aloft and others will cut you down, if you are humble then your virtue will shine. In finding one person good you will only draw comparison that the next is bad. All are equal and have equal opportunity, but many waste it on trivia, intellectual games, material wealth, greed and nonsense. What is their loss?!

If one is inflexible and cultivates only self-motivated activities (personal gain, career, one-sided relationships, etcetera), then one will become very lonely in old age. Think only of yourself and others will think nothing of you. Act only for yourself and others will not act for you, the Tao Te Ching tells us. Cultivate flexibility, observation and a more natural lifestyle and you will tune into your deepest senses, become better acquainted with life and the living, enjoy untold pleasure and joy. You might literally inherit the Earth. This is the TAO and the Yin and Yang.

How is it done?

This book has already told you how, in as succinct a way as possible. Construct your life as you would build a house. The materials that you need are all around you and this little book is but the "introductory manual". The life building process is fairly easy, it takes little but time and the will to succeed.

Firstly, you need a *firm foundation* on which to build. A strong, tall house can not be built on sand! Exercise; T'ai Chi Ch'uan (Supreme Polarity Boxing) is an excellent form of exercise for health suppleness and grounding one's energy, and it makes you think about what you are doing, step-by-step. It is also a form of self-defence and I highly recommend the study of this with a good teacher who can enlighten you as to the why's and wherefore's of the Yin/Yang techniques - NOT just Push Hands games or competition (Competition is unyielding as your intention must be to do better than all others).

Second. Diet comes next. A well balanced diet will set the materials of your foundation. The two elements will make it strong building.

Thirdly, the *walls* of your abode. The Tao Te Ching teaches us that things are only useful for their absence; walls are only useful when there is an absence of it for a door or window. To let in natural light, philosophy and life's experience is essential. As strong as you abode needs to be, even a castle with tall defences, we need to let others in, like we need to open our minds to allow knowledge to flow in.

Fourth, love. As we have said above, love is the key to life. We are bound to meet those on our journey who are inflexible, insensitive, corrupt and unable to give, only take; I have met my share of these and draining as it is, one must get up and open those doors to start again; the last thing you would want, surely, is to become like them. It is easy to be guarded, especially after an attack! The real trick is to learn, let the experience enter and pass through, not let it lodge like a poison arrow in the heart. You cannot lay terms and conditions for others, but set an example, let your feelings be known, fear none but yourself - negativity and retreat. Look life in the face, look it in the eye and be not afraid, be glad that you have found life and take it with both hands as your sustenance.

Fifth, you need a *roof* for your house. The shelter of your knowledge and experience will keep you dry and will give warmth to other travellers on The Way. Do not be afraid to let them in and share your warmth, even if they take fright, steal your most precious possession (trust) and hurl abuse at you. You may be frightened yourself sometimes and show them off, regretting it afterwards. But you will still be on The Way and hopefully the experience will teach them. In my adventure filled days of this life I have seen and heard of many a thief with grudge in their hearts turn into good and helpful citizens in later years!

Is it possible these days?

Yes. All things are possible. If you disregard the hundreds, thousands and even millions of people who are trying so desperately to sell you a space in their vile pit of despair and error by making money out of selling fashions and junk items, stuff which we really do not need at all and (if you think about it) does not make us happy in the long term. This does not mean that we should walk around looking scruffy, or not taking care of our appearance, the opposite is true. We should take care of appearance, both outside and in. Remember that good health (mentally and physically) begins on the inside and not with outward appearances of either the body or our house/toys/cars, et cetera.

Manage only that which you can. Accept the basic that you need to live, do not be greedy or try to use others for your own gains. By putting something useful in to life you may accept that which you take out with a clear conscience. Strive to be like water and as you flow on your journey through life so you serve others, try to help someone on your way; remember, if you only help just one person with a timely deed, help one person to better their pitiful lot, then your life and love have not been in vain.

An old oriental saying:

"It is better to light a candle than to curse the darkness".

Many will always find an excuse to avoid change. Have you ever tried to avoid change, or make new paths in your life? It did not work out too well, did it? There is one thing which is inevitable, one thing which is constant and omnipresent, CHANGE! It is impossible to avoid it, so you may as well adapt to it and follow the shining example that Mother Nature gives us.

The Way.

Follow The Way and you will find home.

The path is wide and the view complete.

Atop highest mountain you'll sit alone,

But in the Market your friends you meet.
M.S. '92©.

Thank you for your interest in this book. It is part of a series which the author was compelled to write after one of the many, many spiritual experiences. So far, these consist of several titles under the Life Force Publishing banner and may include at least another one in the future.

"All journeys begin with one step. I wish you peace, love and a happy life. Thank you for reading this little book. I hope that it has helped you start a new journey."

Professor Myke Symonds Shih-fu.

~

T'IEN TI TAO ACADEMY
www.TTTkungfu.com /

(No Spam Advertising as this is illegal in most places and can lead to large fines for the business responsible!)

The Author's Background

CHIEF INSTRUCTOR; T'IEN TI TAO CH'UAN-SHU

ONLY PERSONAL INVITE STUDENT OF

GRAND MASTER CLIFFORD CHEE SOO

INTERNATIONAL TAOIST ARTS ASSOCIATION &

CHINESE CULTURAL ARTS ASSOCIATION.

[TEACHER'S CHOI KUNG CLASSES 1975 - 1979]

Head Instructor of Ability Martial Arts Association (AMAA)

Instructor's professional Insurance and backing org.

TAOIST STUDIES INCLUDE:

TAOIST PHILOSOPHY

TAOIST K'AI MEN - YOGA

TAOIST CHANG MING DIET

CH'I KUNG & T'AI CHI CH'UAN

TAOIST HEALTH & HEALING ARTS

also
T'AI CHI CH'UAN 12/21/32 STEP SUN STYLE for ARTHRITIS
(with Dr. PAUL LAM)

CHINESE FIGHTING SYSTEMS AND PRINCIPLES,

HISTORY AND THEORY.

INDIAN; YOGA, BUDDHISM, SUFISM.

TIBETAN; BUDDHIST PHILOSOPHY, MEDITATIONS & SPECIAL EXERCISES.

VARIOUS OTHER; ZEN, KEMPO, MASSAGE, DIETETICS, HERBALISM, ETC.

QUALIFICATIONS:

- •Professor of Taoist Arts
- •Master of Arts, B.N.M.A.A.
- •Honours Award for Promotion of Kung-fu in UK
- •Chief Instructor of TTT (Teaching since 1973)
- •Instructor of TCA (Dr. Lam)
- •GNVQ 2 Sports Coaching
- •Taoist Philosophy
- •Taoist K'ai Men Yoga
- •Taoist Ch'ang Ming Diet
- •Ch'i Kung Energy Training
- •Taoist diagnostics, health & healing Arts.

OTHER BOOKS BY THE AUTHOR COMING SOON
By late 2022 most of these books should be available through book shops and have ISBN numbers, available by e-mailing the author with the relevant title and requesting the ISBN - desk@TTTkungfu.com

Searching on-line? Look or ask for the 'Life Force Publishing' prefix!

Life Force - **Qigong & Baduanjin**
(Eight Strands of Silk Brocade) Standardised Set.

Description: The most popular set of Ch'i Kung exercises in the world, now standardised for safety and universal learning ease. Complete and explained exercises with clear illustrations. Plus a special needs section and description for those who are unable to stand up.

Life Force - **T'ai Chi Diet II - Ch'ang Ming** (Long Life Diet)

Description: For many centuries the Chinese Taoists have known the secrets of balanced diet and good health. Foods are like medicine or poison, like herbs (another form of food) it can heal or make ill. Learn how to detect illness or imbalance, how to correct your diet and live longer with more energy. Special needs section covers common illnesses like cancer, migraines, Hypoglycaemia, rheumatism and more.

Life Force - Taoist "K'ai Men" Yoga

Description: K'ai Men means "Open Gate" and refers to the power of this unusual yoga to open the pathways of the intrinsic energies within the body. Each exercise has a warm-up sequence and an extension. It crosses over with Ch'i Kung (energy training) to re-balance and revitalise your whole body and mind.

Life Force - **Practical Philosophy of Tao, for schools and individuals**.

A Letter-sized book ideal for school libraries and teachers who are involved with religions and philosophies. Also a great introduction to the Taoist philosophy used in T'ai Chi Ch'uan and other Arts.

www.ingramcontent.com/pod-product-compliance
Lightning Source LLC
Chambersburg PA
CBHW022022090426
42739CB00006BA/244